One of America's best known professional speakers,
Nido R. Qubein is a very successful businessman and
a highly sought-after consultant to some of the country's top
business leaders. He served as president of the
National Speakers Association and founded several successful
corporations, including Creative Services, Inc. He now
resides in High Point, North Carolina.

GET THE
BEST
FROM YOURSELF

Nido R. Qubein

A SPECTRUM BOOK

Prentice-Hall, Inc., Englewood Cliffs, New Jersey 07632

Library of Congress Cataloging in Publication Data

Qubein, Nido R.
  Get the best from yourself.

  "A Spectrum Book."
  Includes index.
  1. Success. I. Title.
BF637.S8Q42 1983   158'.1   83-10988
ISBN 0-13-407296-0
ISBN 0-13-407288-X (pbk)

ISBN 0-13-407296-0

ISBN 0-13-407288-X (PBK.)

This book is available at a special discount
when ordered in bulk quantities.
Contact Prentice-Hall, Inc., General Publishing Division,
Special Sales, Englewood Cliffs, N.J. 07632.

A SPECTRUM BOOK

Printed in the United States of America

10 9 8 7 6 5 4 3 2 1

Prentice-Hall International, Inc., *London*
Prentice-Hall of Australia Pty. Limited, *Sydney*
Prentice-Hall Canada Inc., *Toronto*
Prentice-Hall of India Private Limited, *New Delhi*
Prentice-Hall of Japan, Inc., *Tokyo*
Prentice-Hall of Southeast Asia Pte. Ltd., *Singapore*
Whitehall Books Limited, Wellington, *New Zealand*
Editora Prentice-Hall Do Brasil Ltda., *Rio de Janeiro*

To my wonderful mother

Victoria Ghawi Qubein

who helped me discover that life really
does work best when it's lived from the
inside out . . . and who clearly showed
me how to get the best from myself in
every worthwhile endeavor I undertake.

CONTENTS

Contents

FOREWORD

Once in a great while, a book manages to successfully blend the widsom of the ages with the practical insights of the present to guide its readers hopefully into the future. *Get the Best from Yourself* does exactly that.

Nido Qubein has captured the wisdom of many of the greatest thinkers and doers of all time to lay a solid foundation for productive and joyful living. Thus, he has reminded us that human beings have a marked advantage over all other of God's creations; we don't have to start over with each generation. We can build upon the rich heritage that has been passed down to us.

But he doesn't stop there. With remarkable insight, he explores the practical knowledge of some of the greatest achievers in his own generation.

Using the tested and proven principles of the past, and the motivational techniques produced by the unfolding knowledge explosion, he offers a valuable formula for personal and professional development.

Nido, himself, is living proof that the American Dream is still very much alive. Here is a young man who came to this country in 1966 from the Middle East. Arriving with virtually no money, with no connections, and with almost no understanding of the English language, he charted a course toward success and personal fulfillment. With minimal help, he worked his way through college, then went on to obtain a master's degree in business.

You see, Nido had an advantage over many native-born Americans. He had been led to believe that America was still the land of opportunity. So he decided to use what he had to the best advantage. Armed with a few slides he'd brought from home, a very limited vocabulary, and a good sense of humor, he put together a short audiovisual program about the Holy Land. He would show the slides and speak, in his broken English, to any church or civic group that would give him an audience. People were captivated by his enthusiasm, his accent, and his humorous stories about being a foreigner in this country.

From that meager beginning, Nido Qubein has become one of the top public speakers in America, averaging more than 200 speaking engagements each year for many of the nation's leading corporations and associations. The people of his own profession thought highly enough of this young man to elect him president of the National Speakers Association, and to bestow upon him that association's highest award.

As a businessman and consultant to industry leaders, he has been highly successful. He achieved his goal of becoming a millionaire by the time he was thirty. He has since set new goals and taken on new challenges.

My friend and colleague, Nido Qubein, has discovered that life really does work best when it's lived from the inside out, and now he tells us how to do it. You'll enjoy this book, again and again.

Norman Vincent Peale

ACKNOWLEDGMENTS

Every worthwhile task of my life has been accomplished with the valuable help of many talented individuals—and the writing of this book is no exception.

First, I am indebted to my wife Mariana who has patiently endured my long trips and my exhausting work schedules—and throughout our life together continues to give me courage, love, and unending support.

Second, to my associate Tom Watson I owe deep gratitude for all the research he has done for this and many other works I have published. But mostly, I'm appreciative for all the hours he has invested listening to me and counseling me in the pursuit of my consulting and speaking career.

Third, to all the great Americans who helped me establish The Nido Qubein Associates Scholarship Fund and who believe in me as a human being, I owe heartfelt thanks.

My greatest debt, however, is to each man or woman who has ever been in my audience when I have spoken, who has heard me on radio during the last dozen years, or who has read or listened to one of my earlier works—for these have stimulated my creativity.

chapter one
THE MAGIC KINGDOM
OF "WHAT IF"

Visit with me, for a few moments, the Magic Kingdom of "What If." Here you can be anything, do anything, have anything, or live any way you wish. It's better than television's "Fantasy Island," because all you have to do is close your eyes and let your imagination wander.

What if you could be anything, or anybody, you chose to be? Think about it! What would you choose to be?

A celebrated athlete?
A famous TV or movie actor or actress?
A powerful political personality?
A wealthy person of leisure?
A strong business leader?
A minister?
A doctor, lawyer, or other professional?

A reporter asked George Bernard Shaw to play the "What If" game, shortly before he died. "Mr. Shaw," he said, "You have visited with some of the most famous people in the world. You've known royalty, world renowned authors, artists, teachers, and dignitaries from every part of the world. If you could live your live over and be anybody you've known, or any person from history," the reporter asked, "who would you choose to be?"

"I would choose," replied Shaw, "to be the man George Bernard Shaw could have been, but never was."

What an insight! The sad fact is that few people ever become all that they could have been. As Robert Browning said, "Of all sad words of tongue or pen; The saddest, these; It might have been."

Yet Shaw realized that, although he might have done even more with his life than he did, he could never be anyone but himself. That realization is the limitation of the Magic Kingdom of "What If". You can choose to become another person only with your imagination. In the real world, you can be only yourself! You can become only the person you are created to be! Yet what you can be is almost unlimited. You are, in many ways, "unique," that is, you are the "only one of your kind."

You Have:
Unique talents and abilities
  Unique opportunities
    Unique mental powers
      A unique personality
        A unique self-image.

The Fact Is That:
No one can do what you can do, exactly as you can do it.
  No one has exactly the same opportunities you have.
    No one knows exactly what you know.
      No one has a personality exactly like yours.
        No one sees you exactly as you see yourself.

Celebrating your uniqueness is fully developing all of the attributes that make you the "one-of-a-kind" person you are.

What If:
All your dreams can come true?
  You can become the person you'd like to be?
    The world is waiting for the unique contribution you can make?
      Life can be as full and rewarding as you hope it can be?

Here are some people who *made* their dreams come true.

As a boy, John Goddard dared to visit the Magic Kingdom of "What If." When he was 15 years old, John Goddard made a list of all the things he wanted to do in life. That list contained 127 goals he hoped to achieve. It included such things as: explore the Nile, climb Mt. Everest, study primitive tribes in the Sudan, run a five-minute mile, read the Bible from cover to cover, dive in a submarine, play "Claire de Lune" on the piano, write a book, read the entire *Encyclopedia Britannica*, and circumnavigate the globe.

Now middle-aged, he has become one of the most famous explorers alive today. He has reached 105 of his 127 goals and done many other exciting things. He is still looking forward to visiting all 141 countries in the world (so far he's visited only 113), exploring the entire Yangtze River in China, living to see the twenty-first century (he'll be 75 years old), visiting the moon, and many other exciting adventures.

Jim Marshall has been described as the most indestructible man ever to play professional football. In a sport where 30 is considered "old age," he played defensive end until he was 42—never failing to start in 282 consecutive games. He is what famous quarterback Fran Tarkenton calls "the most amazing athlete I've ever known in any sport."

Now Jim has had his share of problems. He was once caught in a blizzard in which all of his companions died. Twice he suffered from pneumonia. While cleaning a rifle, he suffered a gunshot wound. He's been in several automobile accidents and has undergone surgery.

The secret of Jim's amazing resiliency is in his two guidelines: "Find a direction and dedicate yourself to that direction, and never realize how high *up* is."

WHAT IS YOUR MOST BASIC FREEDOM?

We talk a lot about freedom these days, but rarely do we exercise our most precious freedom. We all have a type of freedom that we seldom use in a purposeful way. You won't find it in the Bill of Rights or anywhere in the Constitution of the United States. The Declaration of Independence only hints at it. No document of any nation anywhere in the world clearly spells it out. That's because no nation can give it to you, and no nation—no person—can take it away from you.

This freedom is equally available to all people regardless of race, religion, sex, economic status, or circumstance. It is available

to the prisoner, to the invalid, to the poor, to the victim of dis-
crimination, to the timid—even to the citizen of an Iron Curtain
country.

What is this most basic freedom? *Each of us has the freedom to
choose how we will respond to the circumstances in which we find ourselves.*

We Cannot Always Control:
What others do to us
  What happens to us
    Where we are born
      What physical impairments we have
        How much money we start out with
          What others think of us
            What others expect of us
              How high our IQ is

But Each of us Can, and Does, Control:
How we react to what others do to us
  How we cope with what happens to us
    How we live, and if we live, where we are born
      How well we use the physical abilities we have
        What we do with the resources we have been given
          How we respond to the opinions of others
            Whether we can, or will, live up to others' expectations
              What we do with the IQ we have.

Most of the limitations that keep us from realizing our full potential
are artificial. They are imposed on us by circumstances or by other
people.

Artificial Limitations Include:
Our age (we're "too" old or "too" young)
  Empty pockets
    Past failures
      Troubles and pains
        The shortsightedness of those around us
          Lack of education
            Fears
              Doubts

The real limitations that rob us of our freedom to make the best of what we have, and of what we are, have to do with the way we see ourselves and the world around us. Our attitudes hold us back from becoming all that we were created to be.

These Real Limits Include:
A negative outlook on life
Excuses we offer
Our waste of the time we are given
Pettiness
Inflexibility
Feeling sorry for ourselves
Worry
Procrastination
Laziness
Lack of self-discipline
Bad habits

The winners in this world have always been those who have relentlessly used their freedom to choose how they would respond to whatever circumstances greeted them.

For Example:
- Colonel Sanders was "too old" to start a business.
- The Wright brothers knew that no one had ever flown.
- Florence Chadwick knew that others had died trying to cross the English Channel.
- Henry Ford faced a "lack of demand" for his automobiles.
- David was too young, to unskilled, and too poorly equipped to face Goliath.

However, winners have a history of ignoring the shortsighted scoffers and of doing the "impossible." Even the opinions of "experts" were not enough to hold them back.

Consider That:
- After Fred Astaire's first screen test, the memo from the testing director of MGM, dated 1933, said, "Can't act! Slightly bald! Can dance a little!" Astaire keeps that memo over the fireplace in his Beverly Hills home.
- An "expert" said of Vince Lombardi, "He possesses minimal football knowledge. Lacks motivation."

- Someone said of Albert Einstein, "He doesn't wear socks and forgets to cut his hair. Could be mentally retarded."
- Socrates was called, "An immoral corruptor of youth."

FREEDOM NECESSITATES CHOICES

There's so much to see, to do, to be! Life is full of choices—like a giant smorgasbord. Yet here we stand, with our small plates that can hold only so much. Freedom demands that we make choices.

In the Magic Kingdom of "What If," you'll find a blank check. It is drawn on a limitless bank, and it is signed by a loving benefactor who can give you anything you want. All you have to do is fill in your name on the blank marked "Pay to the order of:" Go ahead! Mentally write your name as the payee of the check.

Now, in the "Amount" space, write what you'd like most to have out of life. Go ahead! I dare you! Reach for a star!

Or would you rather just muddle aimlessly through life? Would you rather allow circumstances, or other people, to dictate the way you will spend the remainder of your life? Would you rather "fly by the seat of your pants," letting the myriad of your little decisions wipe out the big decisions that could shape your life as you want it to be?

Who's In Charge of Your Life?

Even a short visit to the Magic Kingdom of "What If" raises a big question: Who's in charge of your life? When you were a child, your parents were in charge of your life.

They Told You:
What time to go to bed
  What time to get up
    What toys you could have
      Even what to eat

Later on, you looked to your teachers and the school principal to tell you what to do.

They Decided:
What you would read
   What you would learn
      When to put your head down and rest
      When you could go to the bathroom
         Even what you could eat

Gradually, your peers began to exercise some control.

They Dictated:
What clothes you would wear
   Where it was "cool" to be seen
      The way you would talk
         Maybe even what you would drink

As you reached young adulthood, you turned to others for guidance as to what you should do.

You:
Talked your plans over with a friend
   Asked a minister for advice
      Talked out your decisions with a counsellor
         Took a job and let the boss decide what you would do.

Living was much simpler when you were little. When you were afraid, Mom or Dad would come into your room. If you asked, they would stay with you, or leave a light on, until you went to sleep. They took responsibility for you.

Now you're all grown up. In the past, if things did not go the way you wanted them to go, you could blame your age, your social status, your job, or your circumstances. But gradually you realized that you could change such things—if you were willing to pay the price to change them. You've spent enough time in the Magic Kingdom of "What If" to believe that there could be more to life than what you have experienced so far. You have begun to suspect that your life is not shaped by the people around you or by the circumstances in which you find yourself. Slowly, it's dawning on you that you are in control of your life. Sure, you can talk with other people and get their advice. But ultimately you must decide. *It's time to face the fact— you are in charge of your life! You are, and always will be a product of your choices.*

The Magic Kingdom of "What If"

Figure 1–1 How're You Doing So Far?

Circle the letter indicating the response that most accurately represents the way you feel at the moment:

1. I like being the way I am: (a) all of the time, (b) most of the time, (c) sometimes, (d) never.
2. I enjoy what I am doing as a profession: (a) all of the time, (b) most of the time, (c) sometimes, (d) never.
3. I accomplish my goals: (a) every time, (b) most of the time, (c) occasionally, (d) never.
4. I have positive attitude about: (a) everything, (b) most things, (c) a few things, (d) nothing.
5. My closest relationship: (a) is ideal, (b) could be improved, (c) needs much improvement, (d) is terrible.
6. My relationships with my fellow workers: (a) are ideal, (b) could be improved, (c) need much improvement, (d) are hopeless.
7. If I keep going the way I am, I will: (a) reach my full potential, (b) do fairly well in relation to my goals, (c) be old before my time, (d) disappoint myself and others.
8. My personal finances: (a) resemble Fort Knox, (b) are ample but not all I desire, (c) are barely adequate, (d) are a disaster.
9. Most of the people I know: (a) owe their success to knowing me, (b) feel enriched by knowing me, (c) find me to be interesting, (d) find me to be a bore.

Score yourself as follows: 10 points for each (a) answer, 7 points for each (b) answer, 5 points for each (c) answer, and 1 point for each (d) answer.

- If you scored 85 to 100 points, stop reading this book and pass it along to a friend.
- If you scored 70 to 84, you've got a lot going for you. This book should help to reinforce your positive attitudes and actions.
- If you scored yourself 55 to 69, like most of us you have some areas that need major improvement. This book could be helpful.
- If you scored 40 to 54, the thoughts expressed in this book could radically change your outlook on life.
- If you scored 39 or less, what have you got to lose? Read on!

Exercise 1–1 might help you to assess how well you're doing at exercising your freedom to respond, in any way you choose, to the circumstances in which you find yourself. It is not a test. It is designed to help you think through how fully in control of your life you are.

You and the Law of Inertia

Were you happy with your score on the questionnaire in Exercise 1–1? If not, consider the *law of inertia*, which says:

> A body at rest tends to remain at rest, and a body in motion tends to remain in motion, at the same speed and in the same direction, unless acted upon by an outside force.

With one major change, that law applies very well to the pattern of our lives.

People:
Who are successful tend to remain successful
  Who are happy tend to remain happy
    Who are respected tend to remain respected
      Who reach their goals tend to go on reaching their goals

So, what's the major change? Physical inertia is controlled by outside forces, but the real changes in the directions of our lives come from inside us. As William James said, "The greatest discovery of my generation is that a person can alter his life by altering his attitude of mind."

You can live every day of your life. You can be alive to the tips of your fingers. You can accomplish virtually any worthwhile goal you set for yourself.

MEANWHILE, BACK IN THE REAL WORLD

The problem with the Magic Kingdom of "What If" is that you can't live there! Those who try, find that it turns into the Deadly Kingdom of "If Only."

They Find Themselves Saying:
"If only I had more money, I could. . ."
"If only my circumstances were different, I could . . ."
"If only my race were different, I could . . ."
"If only I were better educated, I could . . ."
"If only I had not done . . ."

The dreams you discover in the Magic Kingdom of "What If" can come true only when you have both feet planted firmly in the real world. If you visit the Magic Kingdom of "What If" often, dream its lofty dreams, and then return to the real world and make them come true, you'll be amazed at what you can accomplish with your life.

Dare to Be a Practical Dreamer

Dare to dream! Dare to hope! Dare to see yourself as a great big bundle of potential! Psychiatrists are increasingly acknowledging the value of daydreams. Studies have shown that people who have the highest IQs tend to spend a lot of time daydreaming—imagining how things could be. Most of the truly great inventions and developments of history started out as images in the minds of dreamers.

But remember, a dream is only a dream until you make it come true. Ralph Waldo Emerson was one of the greatest visionaries of history. In fact, many consider him the greatest "mystic" who ever lived. Yet Emerson said to an aspiring artist, "There is no way to success in our art but to take off your coat, grind paint, and work like a digger on the railroad, all day, every day." When I was a boy, my mother often said to me, "If it is to be, it is up to me."

For every truly great innovation that has been made, at least a hundred could probably have been made, but they never were. Why? There are two basic reasons: Many potential innovators failed to dream, and many dreamers failed to make their dreams become reality.

Dreams:
Lift our sights from the ordinary to the potential
    Give us hope

>   Inspire us to attempt the impossible
>   Call us to become more than we have been
>   Inspire others to hope for something more
>   Challenge us to grow

Either we dream of bigger and better things, or we fall into the pit described by Henry David Thoreau when he said, "The mass of men lead lives of quiet desperation."

The practical side of dreaming is being willing to pay the price to make those dreams come true.

>   *Practicality:*
>   Gives shape and form to our dreams
>   Makes tangible our hopes
>   Renders our ideas useful
>   Translates our aspirations into actions
>   Adds substances to our ideals

Dreams Come True When You Pay the Price

"Nido, I'd give anything to be able to speak before a group as you do," a young man said to me recently.

"You'd be ten times better than me," I replied, "if you only gave one-tenth what I did."

Each day presents us with a wide array of possibilities and potentialities. Opportunities parade before us like the stars on a cloudless night. People all around us seize them—like the guy who made a fortune on "pet rocks."

"But those people are lucky!" someone moans.

Really? Your dreams can come true when you are willing to pay the price to make them come true.

Many people are not willing to pay the price to be successful. Maybe that's why so many withdraw into what my fellow trainer Jim Newman calls a "comfort zone." They long for a place to rest, a place to be safe, a place to be comforted and coddled.

>   *But "Comfort Zones" are like Caves:*
>   Their darkness makes it hard to see
>   Their stagnant air grows stale and becomes hard to breathe
>   Their walls box us in
>   Their low ceilings keep us from stretching to our full height

The fact that you have read this far indicates that you are not willing to live the remainder of your life in a "comfort zone." Perhaps you are tired of being a loser. Maybe you have been a winner in the "bush leagues," and you are ready to move on up to the "big league" in the game of life.

And that leads us to the next chapter, "What Makes a Winner?"

chapter two
WHAT MAKES
A WINNER?

As you reach out for success, the most important asset you can have is a winner's attitude.

Literature and History Are Full of People Who:
Suffered from severe handicaps
 Often had talents that were inferior to those around them
  Sometimes lived in the worst of circumstances
   Usually faced many defeats

Yet many of those people are listed among the winners in life's Hall of Fame.

Why? What Made Them Achieve?
When others around them failed
 When others had greater talents
  When others had greater opportunities
   When others often had far greater resources

The secret is this: *They had a winner's attitude!*

In the game of life, just as in sports, there are always far more losers than there are winners. In baseball, only two teams can play the annual World Series—and only one of them can win. In professional football, only two teams can make the Superbowl. Almost every professionally played sport in the United States is the same in this respect: Only one team, or one individual can win the big prize!

Horse racing sportscasters use a term that more accurately parallels the game of life. The term is "also ran." After listing the winner and the runners-up of a race, they mention the "also rans." These are the horses that were in the race but that did not do well enough to be listed among the winners. The big prize goes to the winner, and smaller prizes are awarded in descending order to the runners-up. But little or none of the prize money and acclaim goes to the many "also rans."

In business and in human services, there are also a few winners, but many "also rans." A few are the leaders, the outstanding achievers, and the small minority who give the service "above and beyond the call of duty." But sadly most people are only listed as working for an organization or corporation.

The Narrow Margin of Victory

If you carry the horse racing analogy a step further, you will notice something very interesting. Usually, the margin of victory for the winners is not very wide.

For example, a horse named Nashua won more than a million dollars in his racing career. Yet all of Nashua's racing time totaled up to less than one hour. (Of course, that figure doesn't include the endless hours of preparation required to win all those races.) When Nashua was sold, he brought more than a hundred times more money than most of the horses that ran against him.

What makes Nashua a hundred times more valuable than other horses? Is he a hundred times faster than the "also rans?" No! To be a consistent winner, and thus far more valuable, he needed only to run slightly faster than the others. In fact, many of the races Nashua won were won only "by a nose." The judges could not award the prize until they had looked at a picture of the noses of the two front runners going over the finish line.

In every area of human endeavor, the slight edge that separates the achiever from the "also rans" is usually less than 2 percent, according to a writer in a national magazine. More often than not, the winner's slight edge is not talent, resources, or brains. *Usually the deciding factor is the winner's attitude.*

WINNERS MAKE THEIR GOALS: LOSERS MAKE EXCUSES!

My friend Zig Ziglar has helped thousands of "also rans" become winners through his seminars and best-selling book, *See You at the*

Top. In that book, he talks about the "loser's limp." He describes it like this:

In a crucial football game, the home team is down by a touchdown, and time is running out. The wide receiver's number is called in the huddle. He is tired from running down the field all afternoon. His body aches all over from being knocked around by defensive backs. Besides, he knows that the quarterback has been pressured all afternoon, and, with the defense expecting a pass, the odds that the ball will ever be thrown are less than a thousand to one.

So he lopes down the field at about half speed. He makes his cut, and looks for the ball. Much to his surprise, he sees it coming—right on target! The loser makes a heroic leap to attempt the catch, but the ball falls to the ground in the end zone—just beyond his reach. The crowd roars its disappointment.

Slowly, the receiver lifts himself to his feet. Unable to admit that he dropped the ball, he limps toward the sidelines. He's the only person in the stadium who knows he's not hurt. But, knowing that he will not have the crowd's admiration, he settles for their sympathy. He excuses his poor attempt with the "loser's limp."

The moral? *Winners make their goals: losers make excuses!*

Winners:	Losers:
Always have an idea	Always have an excuse
Always say, "I'll do it!"	Always say, "It's not my job!"
See an answer for every problem	See a problem for every answer
Always say, "I can!"	Always say, "I can't!"
Look for a way to do it	Look for a way to get out of it.

Almost always, attitude makes the difference. Whether you think you can or can't, you'll usually be right!

Losers Settle for Second Best!

You can tell the winners from the losers in another way: Winners compare their achievements with their goals, while losers compare their achievements with those of other people.

Richard Petty has won more prize money than any other stock car driver in the history of the sport. His story about what happened when he reported the results of his first race to his mother is an intriguing one.

"Mama!" he shouted as he rushed into house, "there were thirty-five cars that started, and I came in second in the race!"

"You lost!" his mother replied.

"But, Mama!" he protested, "Don't you think it's pretty good to come in second in my first race—especially with so many starters?"

"Richard," she said sternly, "You don't have to run second to anybody!"

For the next two decades, Richard Petty dominated stock car racing. Many of his records still stand, unbroken. He never forgot his mother's challenge—"Richard, you don't have to run second to anybody!"

Winners compare their achievements with their goals and with their own potential. The losers always compare themselves with others.

DO YOU HAVE A WINNER'S ATTITUDE?

Whether you are a success or failure in life has little to do with your circumstances; it has much more to do with your attitude!

Recently, I shared the dinner table with Dr. Norman Vincent Peale as both of us addressed a national convention in New Orleans. This man has inspired a nation, as well as many people around the world, with his books, articles, and inspirational talks. He often says that one of the most common complaints goes something like this: "Dr. Peale, I'd like to start a business, or do something for the good of mankind, but I have no money to start out with!" To that Dr. Peale replies, "Empty pockets never held anyone back. . . . It's only empty heads and hearts that can do that."

You see, losers *blame* their circumstances; winners *rise above* their circumstances. Losers concentrate on the blank wall that boxes them in; winners always look for a way to get under it, over it, around it, or through it.

Do you have a winner's attitude? Check yourself with the questionnaire in Exercise 1–2.

Exercise 2–1. The Winner's Attitude Questionnaire

Put an "X" in the appropriate column after each statement:

	Always	Usually	Seldom
1. I prepare myself adequately for every task.			
2. I view my circumstances positively.			
3. I see problems as opportunities.			
4. I am flexible and tolerant of the views of other people.			
5. I am decisive. I make decisions quickly and act with determination.			
6. I approach every task (no matter how routine) with mental alertness and creativity.			
7. My actions demonstrate that I have faith in God, in myself, and in others.			
8. I am prepared for the worst, but expect and hope for the best.			
9. I am enthusiastic and try to spread enthusiasm to others.			
10. I give every task my best effort.			
11. I confront every fear with personal courage.			
12. I acknowledge that my success is helped by the assistance I receive from others.			
13. I operate with complete honesty, integrity, and sincerity.			
14. I am loyal to those who count on me.			
15. I am committed to excellence in all I do, and take pride in every task I'm asked to perform.			
16. I give more than is expected of me.			
17. I learn from my mistakes and failures rather than allowing them to discourage or defeat me.			

	Always	Usually	Seldom
18. I keep my body in top condition and my energy level high through regular rest, adequate (but not "too" adequate) diet, and a consistent physical exercise program.			
19. I avoid emotional fatigue that comes from worry, pettiness, and holding personal grudges.			
20. I evaluate my performance only against my potential and don't compare my achievements with other people.			
21. I accept responsibility cheerfully.			
22. I welcome new ideas, challenges, and situations.			
23. I am aware that, no matter who I'm working for, I'm my own boss and demand the best from myself.			
24. I concentrate on goals, rather than on activities. I don't waste my time on "busy work."			
25. I am a "team player." I do my best without regard for who gets the credit for what the team accomplishes.			
Totals			

Give yourself 4 points for every "X" in the "Always" column, 2 points for each "Usually" answer; and 0 points for each "Seldom" answer.

- 90 to 100 points: You are well on the way to becoming a winner.
- 80 to 89 points: You have some winning ways but definitely need to read the next section.
- 79 to 80 points: Your attitude is "average." If you want to become a winner, read and carefully study the next section.
- 78 points or less: You could probably benefit greatly from memorizing the remainder of this chapter.

WINNERS ARE MADE—NOT BORN

Earl Nightengale once told the story of a professor who startled a group of college educators with a challenge. He asked them if they could boil down into a brief statement all of the books ever written on how to motivate people. After a long discussion, they came up with the following statement which said it all: "What the mind attends to, it considers; what it does not attend to, it dismisses. What the mind attends to continually, it believes; and what the mind believes, it eventually does." We can all be winners by controlling the input to our great computers—our minds. With enough of the right kind of input, our minds begin to control our emotions—rather than vice versa.

Children are a good example of the "vice versa." Children spend their days looking for things to do, fun to have, ways to entertain themselves and to be entertained by others. Most of us think that children are "cute" because they are growing. We don't expect children to act maturely because they are still children. Yet of people still act like children at 35, we don't think they are either cute or attractive. Why? Because we expect a person to mature with age.

Although maturity involves many things, it certainly includes taking charge of our lives with the mind—through a series of rational decisions—rather than allowing our emotions to rule us. Perhaps this explains why boredom is such a problem in our society. People with adult bodies and minds, who are still ruled by their emotions, can never find enough things—fun and entertainment—to satisfy their cravings. Jesus, the wisest teacher who ever lived, said that a person's life does not consist of the things that he or she possesses. If you are ever bored or dissatisfied with the way your life has been so far, maybe it's time to face up to the fact that *you were born to be a winner*.

YOU'RE A TIGER—NOT A GOAT!

From the Orient comes an ancient story that has been a great inspiration in my life. The mother of a small tiger kitten was killed, and the young tiger was adopted by a goat. For months, the young tiger drank the milk from the kindly goat, played with the young goats in the herd, and tried his best to bleat as the goats did.

But, after a while, things did not go well. Try as he may, the little tiger could not become a goat. He didn't look like a goat, he didn't smell like a goat, he couldn't make sounds like a goat. The other goats became afraid of him because he always played too roughly and was getting so big. The little orphaned tiger began to withdraw into himself, to feel rejected and inferior, and to wonder what was wrong with him.

One day, there was a loud crashing sound! Goats bleated and scattered in a hundred directions! The little tiger was glued to the rock on which he sat!

Suddenly, the most magnificent creature he had ever seen came bounding into his clearing! It was orange, with black stripes, and it had eyes that blazed like fire. It was huge!

"What are you doing here, among the goats?" the intruder asked the little tiger.

"I'm a goat!" replied the young tiger.

"Follow me!" said the huge creature, with an air of authority.

The little tiger followed, tremblingly, as the huge animal wove his way through the jungle. Finally, they came to a large river, and the leader leaned over to drink.

"Go ahead, take a drink," said the huge animal.

As the little tiger leaned over to drink from the river, he saw two of the same animals. One was smaller, but both were orange with black stripes.

"Who is that?" asked the little tiger.

"That's you—the real you!" came the reply.

"No! I'm a goat!" the little tiger protested.

Suddenly, the large animal sat back on its haunches and let out the most terrifying roar the little tiger had ever heard. It shook the whole jungle, and, when it was over, everything became breathlessly silent.

"Now, you do that!" invited the giant animal.

At first, it was hard. The little tiger opened his mouth wide—as he always did when he yawned after filling his stomach with goat's milk. The sound that came out sounded more like a bleat.

"Go ahead!" said the big animal, "You can do it!"

Finally, the little tiger felt something begin to rumble way down in his stomach. Gradually it grew, and grew, and grew, until it began to shake his whole body.

"Roar!!!" he said, when he could no longer hold it in.

"There, now!" said the huge Bengal, "You're a tiger—not a goat!"

The little tiger began to understand why he was discontented playing with the goats. For the next three days, all he did was stalk through the jungle. When he began to doubt he was a tiger, he would sit back on his haunches and let out a roar. It wasn't nearly as strong or as loud as the roar he'd heard from the huge Bengal tiger—but it was enough!

Let me ask you some very personal questions. Are you increasingly discontented with maintaining the status quo? Do you feel you might have what it takes to be a champion? Are you feeling more and more like a major league player in the minor leagues?

If so, perhaps it's time to face the fact that you're a tiger—not a goat! Perhaps it's time you let out that roar and get on with developing a winner's attitude!

How do you develop a winner's attitude? We'll talk about that in the next chapter.

chapter three
THREE STEPS TO BUILDING A WINNER'S ATTITUDE

There are three basic steps to developing a winner's attitude. They are simple to say and easy to understand, but they require more effort than anything you have ever tried.

STEP 1

Make a Strong and Permanent Commitment to Invest Your Life and Talents Only in Those Pursuits That Deserve Your Best Efforts!

If it's worth doing at all, it's worth doing to the best of your ability. If it's not worth the best you can do, it's not worthy of the winner's time.

Since I am often billed as a motivational speaker, I do try to motivate people by sharing things that I have learned from some of the most outstanding winners in history. But I'll let you in on a little secret: Nobody can really motivate another person. That is something that people can do only for themselves!

Anything less than that which calls forth the very best within you will not be important enough to motivate you to overcome all the obstacles that keep you from becoming a winner. When a goal matters enough to a person, that person will find a way—the resources—to accomplish what at first seemed impossible. For example, Alcoholics Anonymous has been highly successful at helping people overcome a most severe habit. Yet, any member of that fine organization will tell you that he or she can do nothing to help an alcoholic—until that person is titally committed to the goal of sobriety.

Only when you are totally committed to an overriding purpose will you put forth the effort required to overcome discouragement, misunderstanding from other people, and defeat. Consider the bumpy career of Abraham Lincoln. He:

- Lost his job in 1832
- Was defeated for the legislature in 1832
- Failed in business in 1833
- Elected to legislature in 1834
- Lost his sweetheart to death in 1835
- Had a nervous breakdown in 1836
- Was defeated for Speaker in 1838
- Was defeated in bid for Congress in 1843
- Was elected to Congress in 1846
- Lost nomination bid for Congress in 1848
- Was rejected for Land Officer in 1849
- Was defeated for Senate in 1854
- Lost nomination for Vice Presidency in 1856
- Was again defeated for Senate in 1858
- Was elected President in 1860.

Only Lincoln's deep conviction that God had given him a mission to fulfill kept him going when most people would have quit. Such motivation might well be ridiculed in this day of glorification of the self—as it was in his day—but it contains the kind of stuff that causes people to become winners.

Of course, people with the winner's attitude know that fame and fortune are not the only measures of success. Public recognition and money are only superficial ways of keeping score. What drives the winners to put forth Herculean effort, to bounce back from failures and defeats, to overcome handicaps, and to battle discouragement and fear, is the knowledge that they are involved in a purpose that is bigger than themselves. Because losers lack the quiet inner strength and motivation that come from a sense of purpose, they

Often Suffer From:
TGIF (thank God it's Friday) blues
    The consequences of constantly being late or absent from work

Emotional fatigue from keeping up with the pace of life
The emptiness of underachieving
Boredom, anxiety, and depression.

Perhaps this inner strength is what Albert Schweitzer, who gave up a lucrative medical practice to spend his life caring for the natives of Africa, referred to when he said: "We must all mutually share in the knowledge that our existence only attains its true value when we have experienced in ourselves the truth of the declaration, 'He who loses his life shall find it.' "

If you want to develop a winner's attitude, the first step is to make a strong and permanent commitment to invest your life and talents only in those pursuits that deserve your best efforts. We will see how to go about choosing those pursuits in Chapter 8.

STEP 2

Make a Strong and Irrevocable Commitment to Give All That You Have, and All That You Are, to Achieve Your Goals!

When asked the secret of his success, Charles Dickens said, "Whatever I have tried to do in life, I have tried with my heart to do well."

That's the difference between winners and losers. Losers do what is required of them, or even less; but winners always do more than is required—and they do it with enthusiasm. Losers are always looking for an easy way out. But winners, having committed themselves to work only toward their chosen goals, roll up their sleeves and take on challenges as they come. The great philosopher Elbert Hubbard once said, "Folks who never do more than they get paid to do, never get paid for any more than they do." Edward Markham put it another way:

> For all your days, prepare;
> And meet them ever alike;
> When you are the anvil, bear;
> When you are the hammer, strike.

Losers see themselves as doing a job Winners see themselves as a part of all humankind and their work as their contribution to a better world. George Bernard Shaw, the great English playwright, put it this way:

> I am convinced that my life belongs to the whole community and as long as I live, it is my privilege to do for it whatever I can, for the harder I work the more I live. I rejoice in life for its own sake. Life is no brief candle for me. It is a sort of splendid torch which I got hold of for a moment, and I want to make it burn as brightly as I possibly can before turning it over to future generations.

What an attitude! Can you imagine life ever being boring, or work dull, for a person with such a spirit?

The winner accepts the fact that problems are only opportunities in disguise. To the winner, everything is opportunity. Edmund Burke declared:

> The battle of life is in most cases fought up hill, and to win it without a struggle is almost like winning it without honor. If there were no difficulties, there would be no success; if there were nothing to struggle for, there would be nothing to be achieved. Difficulties may intimidate the weak, but they act only as a wholesome stimulus to men of resolution and valor. All experience of life, indeed, serves to prove that the impediments thrown in the way of human advancement may, for the most part, be overcome by steady good conduct, honest zeal, activity, perseverance, and, above all, by a determined resolution to surmount difficulties and to stand up manfully against misfortune.

Nothing Works Like Work. Much has been said about STP, LSD, and THC—the escape-from-reality drugs. However, a far more dangerous escape vehicle is much more widespread than these drugs. It is SFN, or SOMETHING FOR NOTHING. For many people, its temptation is almost irresistible. It is frighteningly habit-forming. It destroys self-reliance and self-respect, and, psychologically, it has the guilt-producing impact of receiving stolen goods.

No wonder a leading psychiatrist has said that America is one big identity crisis. To the normal person who wakes up in the morning with nothing useful to do, and with nowhere to go where he or she is needed, life becomes a nightmare out of which that person must make some sense—or go crazy.

Consider these evaluations of work by some of the all-time winners:

Don't be misled into believing that somehow the world owes
you a living. The boy who believes that his parents, or the
government, or anyone else owes him his livelihood and that
he can collect it without labor will wake up one day and find
himself working for another boy who did not have that belief
and, therefore, earned the right to have others work for him.
                                                    —*David Sarnoff*

The common denominator for success is work. Without work,
man loses his vision, his confidence and his determination to
achieve.
                                            —*John D. Rockefeller*

"It's 99% perspiration, and 1% inspiration," when asked to
explain his genius.
                                            —*Thomas A. Edison*

If people knew how hard I worked to get my mastery, it
wouldn't seem so wonderful after all.
                                                    —*Michelangelo*

A genius? Perhaps, but before I was a genius I was a drudge.
                                                    —*Paderewski*

All the genius I have is the fruit of labor.
                                            —*Alexander Hamilton*

You may have the loftiest goals, the highest ideals, the noblest
dreams, but remember this, nothing works unless you do!

Hang in There— No Matter What! Losers are sometimes
known for the projects they start; but winners are remembered by
the projects they complete. B. C. Forbes, founder of *Forbes Magazine*, once said, "One worthwhile task carried to a successful conclusion is better than half-a-hundred half-finished tasks."

Take a Look at These Track Records:
- Henry Ford failed and went broke five times before he finally succeeded.
- Babe Ruth, considered by sports historians to be the greatest athlete
  of all time and famous for setting the home run record, also holds
  the record for strikeouts.
- Winston Churchill did not become Prime Minister of England until
  he was 62, and then only after a lifetime of defeats and setbacks. His
  greatest contributions came when he was a "senior citizen."
- Eighteen publishers turned down Richard Bach's 10,000-word story
  about a "soaring" seagull, *Jonathan Livingston Seagull*, before Macmil-

lan finally published it in 1970. By 1975 it had sold more than 7 million copies in the U.S. alone.
- Richard Hooker worked for seven years on his humorous war novel, *M*A*S*H*, only to have it rejected by 21 publishers before Morrow decided to publish it. It became a runaway best-seller, spawning a block-busting movie and a highly successful television series.

In life's success formula, nothing can take the place of persistence. Talent will not; it is common to find unsuccessful men with outstanding ability. Opportunity will not; many bungle their best chances by dropping the ball too soon. Enthusiasm will not; with the lazy and impatient, it can vanish overnight. Perseverance and determination alone are indispensible when it comes to getting the job done.

If what you are doing is worth doing, hang in there until it is done!

Some Won't Understand, but That's Okay! There will always be critics and skeptics who, unwilling to try themselves, will ridicule and criticize the person who plods on despite the circumstances. Abraham Lincoln was called "a gorilla" and "a buffoon." He was labeled by one of his peers "an embarassment to the republic." I'd tell you who those critics were, but nobody seems to remember their names.

How About These Remarks:
- You're putting an alligator there instead of a shirt pocket? I can't believe it! Those are never going to sell!
- No worries, boss. Nobody's going to buy those little Japanese cars.
- Who on earth would want six bottles of the same thing in a package with a handle on it?
- Those tires sure look flat to me. What did you say they're called? Radials?
- Watches with no hands? You're crazy!
- Oh come on. Don't tell me they can put music on Scotch tape.

About the negative people who always look for something to criticize, the late President Theodore Roosevelt said:

It's not the critic who counts; not the man who points out how the strongman stumbled or where the doer of deeds could have done them better. The credit belongs to the man who is actually in the arena; who strives valiantly; who errs and comes short again and again, because there is no effort without error and shortcoming; who does actually try to do the deed; who knows the great enthusiasm, the great devotion, knows in the end the triumph of high achievement, and who, at the worst, if he fails, at least fails while daring greatly. Far better is it to dare mighty things, to win glorious triumphs even though checkered by failure, than to rank with those poor spirits who neither enjoy nor suffer much because they live in the grey twilight that knows neither victory nor defeat.

If you would develop a winner's attitude, make a strong and irrevocable commitment to give all that you have, and all that you are, to achieve the goals you have selected.

STEP 3
Make a Strong Commitment to Reach Your Full Potential as a Human Being!

Decide, once and for all time, that you will be the best you can be at whatever you set out to do. Vince Lombardi, the lengendary coach of the Green Bay Packers, once gave the following brief but inspiring talk to his team:

> After the cheers have died and the stadium is empty, after the headlines have been written and after you are back in the quiet of your own room and the Super Bowl ring has been placed on the dresser and all the pomp and fanfare has faded, the enduring things that are left are: the dedication to excellence, the dedication to victory, and the dedication to doing with our lives the very best we can to make the world a better place in which to live.

I choose to see myself, and all other humans, as the creative expression of a loving God. In my view, atheistic humanism is at best inadequate and at worst arrogant. The Book of Genesis says that God, the sovereign of the universe, breathed into our nostrils, and gave us life. In other words, each of us contains a part of the Divine. Only when we are committed to excellence can we begin to measure up to all that we were created to be. Only as we see humankind as the product of a Supreme Being can we explain those thousands of daily strivings that call us to become something we have not yet been—those urges to live up to the best within us.

As Emerson would say, only our Maker can lead and teach us what we can do better than anyone else. Only our creator knows the full potential He placed within us.

"Anyone can count the seeds in an apple, but only God can count the apples in a seed," said Dr. Robert Schuller.

If you want the kind of happiness and deep personal satisfaction out of life that circumstances cannot destroy, search until you find what you can do best, what no one could pay you enough money not to do, what you would gladly pay for the privilege of doing. Then do it with all that is within you.

Consider who you are! You were born for greatness, because you were born from greatness. Consider, for a moment, some of the unique capabilities you possess as a human being.

The Ability to Think. Of all the creatures in the earth, only humans have such an enormous capacity to think, to reason, to store massive amounts of knowledge, to develop wisdom, to evaluate, and to view information in a variety of combinations. Yet scientists tell us that even the geniuses, like Einstein, Socrates, and Edison, used less than 10 percent of their mental capacities. As you reach out to develop your full potential, here are some tips that can help you unlock your tremendous mental powers:

1. *Keep your mind uncluttered.* Practice ridding your mind of all negative, self-defeating thoughts.
2. *Practice mental alertness.* Your mind grows with exercise. Keep your mental radar working full time.
3. *Cultivate your reasoning powers.* Make a game of putting what you know into new combinations.
4. *Feed your mind.* Read, listen, and observe everything you can. Always make sure that you understand your mental input.
5. *Cultivate curiosity.* Ask questions about things you don't understand. Never be satisfied with what you know. Develop your imagination.
6. *Organize your thoughts.* Practice going from what you know, to discover what you don't know.
7. *Be open.* Never dismiss an idea as useless. Listen to viewpoints that are different from yours. You can learn something from everv person you meet.
8. *Practice Objectivity.* Always be willing to examine an idea or bit of information from a variety of viewpoints.
9. *Discipline your mind to work for you.* Make it do what you want it to do, when you want it to do it.

10. *Cultivate common sense.* True wisdom is in knowing what to do with what you know. Learn to balance everything you know against the values that have meaning to you.

"I know of no more encouraging fact." said Thoreau, "than the fact that thought is a sculptor who can create the person you want to be."

The Ability to Create. The human mind, coupled with an indomitable spirit and a marvelous physical body, is capable of creating in a way that is unknown anywhere in the universe. Even when the physical body is limited in certain key areas, the human mind and spirit can break free to create in the most amazing ways.

Consider Helen Keller, who has to be one of the most marvelous people I was ever privileged to meet. Born blind, deaf, and mute, she was cut off from the most vital links of communication with all other humans. Yet her keen mind and unconquerable spirit enabled her to write 27 books, as well as to inspire people all over the world to become more than they were.

If you would reach your full potential, cultivate all of the creative urges within you, and respond to the sensitivity that cries out for expression. Develop your best and most useful skills to their maximum level.

The greatest enemy of your creative powers is smug complacency—being satisfied with less than what you are capable of doing. In St. Peter's Cathedral, in Rome, there is an incredibly lifelike statue of Moses. On one knee of that statue is a chip in the stone. Asked how it got there, a guide explained that it was placed there in frustration by the sculptor, Michelangelo. When the sculptor had finished his work, he looked tearfully at the statue, threw his hammer, and screamed, "Why dost thou not speak?"

Of course, no one ever becomes perfect, but anyone can improve. This urge to create, and to improve our creative abilities, gives us our best reason to grow—and to keep on growing.

The Ability to Love. Human beings have both an overwhelming capacity to love and an overriding need to love and be loved. We need to reach out and to get into touch with other human beings. This urge expresses itself as soon as we draw our first breath, and it remains a part of our makeup until we draw our last breath.

Of all the human abilities, love is the most noble and the most enobling. It is by far the most powerful force in the universe. Love moves the spirit to create, the mind to think, and the body to perform. Hate may be a strong force, as are self-centered egotism and fear. However, nothing can lift you to the heights enjoyed by those who respond to the love within and the love from others. Only love can make all your success worthwhile. Whatever else you cultivate, cultivate love. Only when you love and are loved can you reach your full potential as a human being.

The Ability to Laugh and Cry. As far as we know, humans are the only animals in the universe with the delicate emotional structure that enables them to laugh and to cry. To reach our full potential we need to do both. "A merry heart doeth good like a medicine: but a broken spirit drieth the bones," says the writer of Proverbs.

Experts on stress point out that a good sense of humor is a strong defense against being overcome by tension. The person who can laugh often, and who finds humor in even the most stressful events, can keep going when others are falling beside the way. People enjoy being around those who have a good sense of humor.

Weeping is also a part of the human experience. The loss of a loved one, the agony of defeat, severe disappointments, and many other circumstances bring sorrow to all of us. The key to emotional health is to learn how to handle grief. The person who reacts to sorrow only with anger becomes embittered, hardened, and cynical. Someone has said that tears wash the soul. I like the way Harry Emerson Fosdick put it: "Life asks not merely what can you do; it asks how much can you endure and not be spoiled." It was a wise old sage who said, "Life is a grindstone: whether it grinds you down or polishes you up depends on what you are made of."

We often quote the first part of Ella Wilcox's poem, "Laugh and the world laughs with you." But the remaining lines offer an important reminder about how to deal with sorrow and pain:

> *Weep, and you weep alone;*
> *For the sad old earth must borrow its mirth;*
> *But has trouble enough of its own.*

Laughter is a gift to be shared with all, but tears can best be endured alone—or with a friend who willingly shares our grief.

The Ability to Make Ethical and Moral Judgments. Other animals respond to innate drives, but humans have the capacity to make ethical and moral judgments. Call it conscience, values, or whatever you will, something in all of us rises up at times and says, "This is good!" or "This is bad!" And we ignore it at our own peril.

William Faulker once gave some very good advice to a student: "I have found that the greatest help in meeting any problem with decency and self-respect and whatever courage is demanded is to know where you yourself stand. That is, to have in words what you believe and are acting from."

Ideas about morality are constantly changing, and the ways of coming to those moral judgments have been discussed in countless books. It is such a complex subject that many people simply choose not to face up to what it means to them. However, even that option is a moral judgment.

The Ability to Receive and Leave Behind a Heritage. Animals have to start from scratch with nothing but what they have inherited through their genes. A glorious part of the creative genius of humans, however, is that we have the ability to transmit knowledge and wisdom from one generation to the next. Humans have that unique ability to make their lives better by building on the vast storehouse of wisdom and knowledge that has come down to us through the ages. A few minutes at a public library can open to you the wisdom of the philosophers, to the romance of the poets, or to the knowledge of the scientists—even from centuries ago. Isn't it nice to know that you don't have to reinvent the wheel, rediscover fire, or develop a language? It is humbling to realize that most of the products of our lifetime are possible only because of the strivings and creative genius of those who have gone before us.

It is equally humbling to realize that what we do today will affect the lives of people for centuries to come. We, in turn, can pass along to our children, and to others, that which we have learned.

If you would reach your full potential as a human being, gratefully accept the heritage of the past, build on the wisdom of the ages for the present, and resolve to leave the world a better place than you found it.

Figure 3 –1. Three Steps to a Winner's Attitude

How do you develop a winner's attitude? Make these three vital commitments and, having made them, renew them with every new day!

1. Make a strong and permanent commitment to invest your life and talents only in those pursuits that deserve your best efforts!
2. Make a strong and irrevocable commitment to give all that you have, and all that you are, to achieve your goals!
3. Make a strong commitment to reach your full potential as a human being!

Remember the words of Adlai E. Stevenson: "So live—decently, fearlessly, joyously—and don't forget that in the long run it is not the years in your life but the life in your years that counts."

chapter four
MIRROR, MIRROR, ON THE WALL . . .

Dr. Joyce Brothers, syndicated author and television personality, often says that, "It is no exaggeration to say that a strong positive self-image is the best possible preparation for success in life." Many of America's leading psychologists agree with her on that point, observing that low self-esteem is the root cause of most of the nation's social problems. Your mental image of yourself forms the very core of your personality. It determines more about you than any other single factor affecting your life.

WHY IS SELF-ESTEEM SO CRUCIAL?

Why is the mental picture you hold of yourself so crucial a factor in determining how far you will go in life and how happy you will be along the way?

Your Self-Esteem Shapes:
Your choice of mate
  Your choice of career
    Your choice of friends
      Your choice of leisure activities.

Your Mental Image Determines:
Your attitudes toward yourself and the people around you
  Your capacities to grow and learn
    Your actions and reactions
      Your happiness or lack of happiness.

The Way You See Yourself Has a Profound Impact On:
Your family relationships
  Your career relationships
    All your relationships in worship, play, and community.

Your Two Most Vital Questions

At every major milestone in your life, you can profitably ask yourself two vital questions.

1. Do I really, really like myself?
2. Do I see myself as a capable person and what I am doing as worthwhile?

Since the later chapters focus on the second question, let's zero in on the first question: "Do I really, really like myself?"

Before you jump to a quick answer—that, of course, you like yourself—you should consider some facts.

Professional Counsellors Tell Us That:
- Most people respond quickly that they like themselves, only to discover on further probing that they do not like themselves.
- Many people who start out liking themselves gradually lose their high self-esteem.
- Most people have at least one area of their lives in which they dislike themselves, and that dislike affects their whole lives.
- Many forces in our society conspire against our self-image.
- Countless studies have shown that, if you have high self-esteem, you have it made.

There is mounting evidence that the fully functioning person can be distinguished from the person who just flounders through life by one crucial difference—high self-esteem. In fact, the inner force of self-esteem either propels a person to success and happiness, or it drags that person down to failure as a human being.

Consider These Two Critical Points:
1. If you have high self-esteem, you have nothing to lose, and much to gain, by boosting your self-image even higher.
2. If you have low self-esteem, you can boost your chances for success and personal happiness by raising your value in your own eyes.

WHAT IS A GOOD POSITIVE SELF-IMAGE?

It is easy to point a finger at the bums in the skidrows of major cities, at the chronically depressed people in mental hospitals, at the hopeless drug addicts, and at the countless people in prisons. Those people obviously have poor images of themselves. What is not so easy is determining which of the people you encounter in the everyday world are motivated by strong feelings of their own value. The hardest thing to do is to look within yourself and see how you really feel about yourself.

A Good Positive Self-Image Is Not:

1. Self-Centered Egotism! Someone has said that, "The smallest package in the world is a person all wrapped up in himself." In fact, if you want a formula for becoming miserable, the first ingredient is to *think only of yourself.* People who think only of themselves, and what they want, find it hard to be happy with anything they get. For them, gaining the cooperation of the others who are so vital to their success is almost impossible. Most of their personal relationships are frustrating and disappointing. Mental depression is the constant lot of those who feel they are the most important people in the world. The ultimate expression of self-centeredness is the loneliness and despair that drives a person to suicide. Show me a self-centered person, and I will show you a person who is driven by a poor, negative self-image!

2. Personal Complacency and Smug Self-Satisfaction! You can bet your bottom dollar that the person who flits around from job to job and from relationship to relationship is unwilling to put his or her self-image on the line. Every human relationship involves risk, and those who have a strong positive self-image are willing to risk being hurt or failing in their efforts to become all that they can be.

3. Disdain for Other Persons! People who have strong positive self-images don't look down their noses at people who don't have the advantages they have, or who don't achieve the status and recognition they do. One of the oldest mistakes of the people with low self-esteem is the belief that they can elevate themselves by tearing others down.

A Good Positive Self-Image Is:

1. Accepting Yourself as the Person You Are! Comedian Flip Wilson rose to fame largely through his character, Geraldine, who was always saying, "What you see is what you get!" When Geraldine delivered that line, it was funny—but it's not a bad attitude for a person to develop.

Total, unconditional acceptance of yourself is the first step in building a good positive self-image. All of us have characteristics we don't particularly like about ourselves—things we can do nothing about. Maybe, we think, our nose is too long, our eyes are too close together, or we are too short or too tall.

Why feel like you are second-rate because you are not perfect? Nobody is absolutely ideal, so why should you try to be? "Nobody's perfect. . . . But parts of me are excellent," said the sign on a T-shirt worn by a shapely young lady. The idea reflected by that sign offers a good basis for accepting yourself as you are. I would bet that parts of you *are* excellent! As you focus on the strong elements of your personality, of your body, and of your aptitudes, you have a basis for building a good positive self-image. Accept yourself as the unique, wonderful person that you are—then move on from there.

2. Holding Warm and Non-judgmental Regards for Other People! People who feel good about themselves realize that comparing ourselves with other people is a losing proposition. It is a mark of maturity to allow God to be as original with other people as He is with us. When you accept yourself totally, you are free to accept other people. In fact, one of the surest tip-offs to the insecure personality is a mistrust, or general disliking, of other persons.

3. A Willingness to Risk! Someone noted that the lobster has to shed its shell and grow a new one, if it to grow. The process of growing and learning always involves risk. The person who reaches out to form new relationships, or to deepen existing relationships, runs the risk of getting hurt. A new job, a new location, a new situation might hold many dangers to the happiness and fulfillment of a person, but the positive person is willing to weigh more heavily the possible gains. Those with a strong self-image realize that the only way to keep from making mistakes is to do nothing—and that's the biggest mistake of all!

4. Finding Positive Ways to Express Your Individuality! I once read a sign that said: "Be who you is, 'cause when you ain't who you is, you is who you ain't!" While speaking in Greece recently, a professor told me about an ancient god, Prometheus, who was such a trickster that he could change into any person he chose to be. He changed into so many different people, that he eventually forgot who he was. People who accept themselves are not preoccupied with what others think about them. They are willing to express those traits and inner feelings that give them their uniqueness, without an undue regard for what anyone else thinks. People with strong positive self-images are satisfied to be themselves, regardless of what anyone else thinks about them.

5. Being Self-Reliant and Self-Determinating! People who feel good about themselves realize that they cannot blame their troubles or shortcomings on any person, circumstance, or system. They look within themselves for answers as to how things got a certain way and how things can be changed for the better. You won't find them fixing the blame. You'll find them drawing on their internal resources to find solutions. They will graciously accept help, but they are far more concerned about giving it. They are not as likely to be found talking about freedom, as they are just being free.

SELF-ESTEEM MAKES LIFE
WORTH LIVING, NOW

"Most people are about as happy as they make up their minds to be," said Abraham Lincoln. My observation of people leads me to regard that statement as true. But I would take it a step further, adding that most people are about as successful as they make up their minds to be.

Beat the Classic Conflict

The struggle between success and happiness is such a popular notion that it has become a classic plot for stories, plays, and movies. You've seen them, I'm sure!

They Feature Such Themes As:
The hard-nosed executive who loses his family in his quest for success

The actor or dancer who chooses career over love
The mother who is torn between a career and her children
The retired person who loses his/her reason to live.

In the classic struggle, you can have only one thing or the other—success or personal happiness.

But there is a way you can beat the classic struggle! It is simply this: *Write personal happiness into all your plans for success!* You can see what I mean in my own definition of success:

> Success is finding and doing to the best of your ability, in each moment of your life, what you enjoy most doing, what you can do best, and what has the greatest possibility of providing the means to live as you would like to live in the relation to yourself and all persons you value.

Life is too short for you to settle for second-best in your career, in your personal life, or in any of your significant relationships. Any goal that does not take into account all three areas is not worthy of your pursuit.

Someone said that the good life has three ingredients: learning, earning, and yearning. I am increasingly convinced that maturity is a successful balancing of these three elements.

Beat the Classic Myths

One classic myth is that a person will "find" happiness at a future time—a "magic moment"—and usually in a distant place. Yet, as the famous psychiatrist Victor Frankl said, "The search for happiness is self-defeating." Those who spend their lives searching for happiness never find it, while those who search for meaning, purpose, and strong personal relationships find that happiness usually comes to them as a by-product of those three things.

Happiness is a state of mind and heart that grows from the inside out, not vice versa. The only way that you can find circumstances and relationships that will make you happy is to make up your mind to be happy—whatever your circumstances or the problems in your relationships.

The victims of this myth are so unfulfilled by the experiences of the past, and so anxious over the future, that nothing in the present moment makes living it worthwhile. As one person expressed this feeling, "No matter where I am, I always have the

feeling that my reason for being there is to get somewhere else."
The common word for this feeling is *boredom*, and it is so widespread that the National Institute of Mental Health has termed it
"epidemic."

While boredom with the present moment is widespread, it is
not new. Centuries ago, Goethe wrote about a man who traded his
soul for one moment of time that would be so pleasant that he
would invite it to "linger." What a fool he turned out to be! He not
only lost his soul, as the story goes, but he made a bargain that is
not necessary for any of us to make.

You can beat the "future magic moment" myth through a
very simple technique. Learn to receive each moment, as it comes
to you, as a special and unique gift from God. Celebrate and enjoy
that special moment and use it to shape the future. Remember, the
past is gone forever, and the future can be influenced only by your
actions in the present. So learn how to treasure each moment as it
comes, and leave the past and future in the hands of a loving God.

Another classic myth is that obtaining a position, making a
discovery, doing a deed, or being given something will make a
person a success. Like Willy Loman in Arthur Miller's play, "The
Death of a Salesman," some believers carry this myth to ridiculous
and tragic lengths. Poor Willy was always going to make that "big
sale," bring home the fortune, and gain the recognition he truly
deserved. At last, all he could hope for was that his family would
see what a success he was when countless people showed up for
his funeral. Unfortunately, the only people who showed up to
send Willy off into the afterlife were the people who had loved him
and accepted him as he was.

The only way to beat the "grand-slam myth" is to make the
most of every moment available to you as it becomes available. The
important sale is the one you are attempting to make now! The big
break you are looking for is the opportunity that presents itself
now! Your best bet for a good job is to do the best you can with the
one you have right now! Jesus taught that those who do well with
what they are given will be given more. Success comes to most
truly successful people as a series of little successes, rather than as
one big break. Nobody's going to hand success or happiness to you
on a silver platter. Success seldom comes quickly, and it almost
never comes easily. Most of us miss our best opportunities in life
because they come to us disguised as hard work.

chapter five
HOW TO GROW A STRONG, POSITIVE SELF-IMAGE

Your parents, your environment, other people, and the events of your life all strongly influence the way you see yourself. Ultimately, however, no combination of events and circumstances can determine the image you hold of yourself. What shapes our self-images is not so much what happens *to* us, as what happens *in* us. In this chapter, we will talk about how you can shape a strong positive self-image.

A strong positive self-image can give you the character to face any obstacle that stands in your way. With high self-esteem, you can meet the most disappointing and discouraging situations with faith, hope and courage.

It's this simple! If you like yourself, believe in yourself, and trust your own experiencing process, you can be both successful and happy. You can walk right up to life and become all that you were created to be.

So, how do you grow a healthy, positive self-esteem? Here are some pointers I have found useful. They are not original with me but have been gleaned from some of the greatest minds the world has ever known.

POINTER 1
Start with an Absolute Assurance That God Loves You!

Those who base their lives on the belief that a loving God is acting in their behalf tend to see problems as opportunities for growth.

One psychiatrist observed that Jesus had the "best-organized ego system in the history of the world" because it was structured around a deep personal relationship with His Father. As a result, the armed guards, not their captive, fell to the ground that fateful night in Gethsemane.

"There is a God-shaped vacuum in each of us," said Blaise Pascal. How we will fill that vacuum is our choice, but I have noticed two important things about the way people relate to it: First, those who seek to satisfy their deep inner longings with excitement, their own achievements, and recognition seem to struggle with life as if it were an enemy to be conquered. Second, those who put God at the center of their lives seem to find the joy, hope, and peace of mind that enables them to flow with life and see it as a friend to be welcomed. In short, a strong awareness that you are loved by God provides the most solid foundation for building high self-esteem.

POINTER 2
Accept Yourself Totally and Unconditionally, Starting Now!

What matters is not so much how you got to be the way you are now, but what you do with the person you have become. There is nothing helpful in blaming your parents, the way society has

Exercise 5–1. Self-Acceptance

If you are really serious about becoming both successful and happy, pause to do the following exercise:

1. Make a list of at least ten positive attributes you possess. Be generous, but honest, in listing things you like about yourself. When your list is complete, write a brief expression of gratitude to God, to people who have helped you, and to yourself for the beauties you see in yourself.
2. Make a list (any length) of things you don't like about yourself. Again, be honest. Put a check mark beside the things you feel you can change. Write two brief paragraphs: One should be an acceptance speech acknowledging the things you don't like but can't change; the other, a pledge to change all the things you can.
3. Write a short personality profile describing the person you have indentified yourself to be. Give full attention to both your strengths and limitations.
4. Write a short speech accepting the gift of yourself.

treated you, your physical or mental limitations, or anything else for things you don't like about yourself.

The Real Issues Are:
Who are you?
What are you going to do with yourself?

The starting point for building a strong self-esteem is right now! Accept yourself, and go on from there! Once you have completed Exercise 5–1, you are ready to move on to the next step.

POINTER 3
Quit Saying All Those Mean
and Ugly Things About Yourself!

You don't like it much when someone puts you down, do you? You especially don't like negative comments when they are false, or only half true, right? Yet one word of destructive *self*-criticism does about ten times as much damage to your self-esteem as a word of criticism from *someone else*! People who continuously say bad things about themselves eventually come to believe what they say. Once they believe themselves, they act on their beliefs. They become the nowhere people that they have told themselves they are.

But this phenomenon has another side! When people feed positive thoughts and evaluations about themselves into their minds, they begin to believe those things. They become the exciting people they have told themselves they are. Positive evaluations —compliments to yourself from yourself—are something your self-esteem can grow on.

You cannot ignore all criticisms that you or other people make. If you haven't taken a bath in a week, and you whiff your own B.O., ignoring your nose and the clothespins on your friends' noses is stupid! Learn to evaluate criticisms as destructive or constructive. When you or someone else has a negative comment, decide if you can, and/or should, do something about it.

The point is don't make a habit of devaluing yourself by undue criticism. Make it a habit to say nice things about yourself, to yourself. You'll find that you like yourself better.

POINTER 4
Go to Work on
the Things You Need to, and Can, Change!

Remember the check marks beside the things that you didn't like about yourself but that you could change? Get to work changing them.

In addition, here is a list of things you'd like yourself a whole lot better without:

- *Root out all pettiness and vengeance!* These tendencies are like weeds in a garden: You don't need to study where they come from or how they grow—just pluck them up by the roots and get rid of them. Make it a regular practice to decide whether something is worth getting upset over. Disraeli was once asked how he could appoint one of his most vocal critics to a high position. He replied, "I never trouble myself to be avenged!" Like Abe Lincoln's philosophy was, "I will not allow any man to reduce my soul to the level of hatred." Grudges are like tumors; they can live and grow only when they're eating on you!
- *Declare war on dishonesty!* People who have low self-esteem resort to lies to bolster their images. But lies have the opposite effect: They lower self-esteem, whether they are detected or not! Lying and cheating are nasty habits that rob us of self-respect. They are good for nothing but to be shot on sight!

Interestingly, the opposite is true. Integrity breeds high self-esteem—and it earns you a lot of friends as well.

- *Make habits work for you, not against you!* A habit is nothing but an action that has become automatic. Do almost anything often enough, and it becomes a habit. We can choose our habits as we do our food—and with similar results. Just as our bodies become what we eat, our minds and emotions become the products of the habits we develop.

POINTER 5
Learn to Accept Other People as They Are
and Hold Them in High Esteem.

Earl Nightengale was right on target when he said that 85 percent of the people who are dismissed from their jobs are fired because they can't get along with other people. "Getting along" relies heavily on accepting people as they are. The greatest single source of conflict is one person, or one group, forcing values and expectations on another person or group. Helen Keller wisely said, "Tolerance is the first principle of community; it is the spirit which conserves the best that all men think." It is a real mark of maturity to be forgiving of the faults of others as well as equally enthusiastic about their successes and strong points.

The key to your success, in almost any field, is to be sensitive enough to understand what other people want, and generous enough to help them get it. If you help other people become successful in fulfilling their dreams, you can fulfill your own dreams. And you'll pick up many friends along the way. On the other hand, if you want a formula for failure and personal misery it is simply this: Try to please everybody, and expect everybody to try to please you.

Fixing the blame is never important, and fixing the relationship is never unimportant. Accept the fact that all of the people in every situation have strong and weak points, just as you do; then move on from there. "Do unto others as you would have them do unto you," is still the best foundation for building good relationships.

POINTER 6
Adopt a Positive Mental Attitude and Seek out Positive People!

There are two kinds of people in the world—positive people and negative people. Optimistic, positive persons jump out of bed in the morning and say. "Good morning, Lord!" Pessimistic, negative persons pull the covers up over their heads and moan, "Good Lord, it's morning!" Which kind of person are you?

Whether you are an optimist or a pessimist, the choice as to how you will be in the future is yours, and yours alone. If you are like the people who aren't happy unless they are miserable, you can stay that way. If you want to be joyful, enthusiastic, and excited about life, you can be, regardless of your circumstances.

The first rule of developing a positive mental attitude is: *Act positively, and you will become positive!* You can't *think* your way into *acting* positively, but you can *act* your way into *thinking* positively.

The second rule of developing and maintaining a positive mental attitude is to *seek out people who have positive mental attitudes, and spend most of your time with them!* People do affect our outlook. For example, once a man was about to jump off a high bridge and commit suicide. Another man came along, and the two sat down to talk. After about an hour, both of them jumped off the bridge.

In fact, many people conspire to give us a negative outlook on life. The nature of news reporting is such that we hear much more about the bad than the good. We always hear about the plane that crashes, not about the thousands of planes that land safely. Even weather reporters warn us of a 10-percent chance of rain, instead of a 90-percent chance of a beautiful day!

When you spend time with successful people, with positive people, they reinforce your positive attitudes about life. People who respect themselves and their abilities help you feel good about yourself and your abilities. So if "misery loves company," let 'em have it! Spend your time with people from whom you can draw strength and to whom you can give strength.

POINTER 7
Clarify Your Values, and Keep Them in Focus!

People who are happy and successful learn to value people and to use things. People who are looking for something to make them happy, somehow never seem to find it. Yet those who find a way to be happy while they are looking for something benefit in two ways. Not only are they usually happy while they are looking, but also they typically find what they are looking for. "He only is advancing in life whose heart is getting softer, whose blood warmer, whose brain quicker, whose spirit is entering into living peace," said John Ruskin.

The Hebrews' understanding of idols and idolatry might help you to clarify your own perspective. The ancient Hebrews used the terms "idol" and "idolatry" to symbolize misplaced values. To them, an idol was an imposter—someone who was trying to pass himself off as the "real thing." Idolatry was falling for the fake. When we "idolize" an unrealistic image of ourselves, we cannot possibly like and be happy with the real persons we are. Likewise, when we carve out a niche for ourselves in our imagined future, and decide that we won't be happy until we achieve it, we can only feel threatened and anxious over anything that stands in our way.

As you seek to maintain a positive self-image, remember this rule: *You and the people you love are important. Your goals and actions are only the ways you express your values, and the things you accumulate along the way are life's extras.*

POINTER 8
Be Self-Reliant but Helpful to Others!

The people with the strongest self-esteem are those who have learned to stand on their own two feet. They are willing to pass up the fun-for-the-moment and select a course that pays off in the long run. All of us yearn to be free, and our best chance of remaining free is through self-reliance. Someone said, "He who pays the fiddler, calls the tunes." Only when we are self-reliant can we maintain our self-respect and keep open our widest options. I could not express this idea as well as Ralph Waldo Emerson in these lines:

> There is a time in every man's education when he arrives at the conviction that envy is ignorance; that imitation is suicide; that he must take himself for better, for worse, as his portion; that though the wide universe is full of good, no kernel of nourishing corn can come to him but through his toil bestowed on that plot of ground which is given him to till. The power which resides in him is new in nature, and none but he knows what that is which he can do, nor does he know until he has tried.

At the same time, people who have a positive self-image tend to be genuinely helpful to other people. In fact, the two tendencies go together so well that it is hard to tell which produces the other. It is probably a little bit of both. Those who feel good about themselves long to help others feel good about themselves, and the more they reach out to help others, the better they feel about themselves. Only the insecure, the frightened, the people with low self-esteem approach life with an attitude that says, "It's every man for himself!" Sadly, they find only more insecurity and lower self-esteem.

There are two seas in the Holy Land. The Sea of Galilee takes in fresh water from a brook, uses it to produce a wide variety of marine vegetation life, and then gives it to the Jordan River. The Jordan, in turn, spreads the life down throughout the desert and turns it into fertile plain. While the Sea of Galilee bustles with life, the Dead Sea is exactly that—a dead sea. Its water is so full of salt that it cannot sustain life. Why? It takes in the water from the Jordan River and hangs on to it. It has no outlet.

What a perfect picture of the differences in people. Those who "get all they can and can all they get" tend to become self-centered and afraid that someone will steal from them. But those who give freely of themselves usually end up having more than they can give away. Robert Louis Stevenson expressed it like this:

> To be rich in admiration and free from envy; to rejoice greatly in the good of others; to love with such generosity of heart that your love is still a dear possession in absence or unkindness— these are the gifts of fortune which money cannot buy and without which money can buy nothing. He who has such a treasury of riches, being happy and valiant himself, in his own nature, will enjoy the universe as if it were his own estate; and help the man to whom he lends a hand to enjoy it with him.

· POINTER 9
Cultivate a Strong Sense of Gratitude!

Someone once said that the biggest joke in the world is a "self-made" person. Such an individual does not exist. Likewise, the greatest tragedy in the world is the person who arrogantly professes, "Nobody ever gave me anything!" Whether that person is materially rich or poor, he or she is suffering from poverty of soul.

Once, in the early days of my public speaking career, when I was feeling particularly proud of my accomplishments, I experienced one of the most humbling events of my life. I was in Albany, Georgia to address a group of very successful people. It was "big stuff" to a youngster who only a few years earlier could speak absolutely no English!

On the morning of my scheduled address, I arose early, excitedly went to the window to greet the day, and opened my mouth to say my usual, "Good morning, Lord!" But not a sound came out! I tried again, but still I could not speak! Now, a public speaker with laryngitis is about as helpless as a centipede with sore feet! In my panic, I wondered what I would do!

As I sat on the edge of the bed and struggled to speak above a whisper, something far deeper began to dawn on me. I had taken so much for granted! Suddenly, I found myself on my knees, whispering a prayer of thanks to God for all the many things he had given me! I learned that, sometimes, you have to lose something before you realize where it comes from. My voice soon returned, and with it came a new awareness of just how much I have received from a loving God.

People who have a strong positive self-esteem are truly humbled when they realize how much God has given them. They are awed by the contributions others have made to their lives. Bishop Gerald Kennedy said:

> The greater a man is, the more humble he is as he remembers the faith, the dream, the hope, that made his life possible. If any man is tempted to pride because of his accomplishments, let him remember what he has received from all those people of the past. It was their faith that set the direction of his life, and the best he can strive for is to become the fulfillment of their faith.

Yet, gratitude does not come automatically; it has to be cultivated. Many people never really feel or express it. For example, when the *Lady Elgin* collided with a lumber barge and sank on a stormy night in 1860, 393 people were left stranded in the waters of Lake Michigan. In all, 279 of them drowned. Edward Spencer, a college student, plunged into the water again and again to rescue people. After he had pulled 17 people from the water, the strain overcame him and he collapsed, never to stand again. For the remainder of his life, he was confined to a wheelchair. Years later, someone asked him his most vivid memory of that fateful night. "The fact that not one of the 17 ever returned to thank me," was his reply, according to a Chicago newspaper. It is unthinkable that no one saw fit to say thanks, even for his or her life

Perhaps gratitude does not come easily for most people because focusing our attention on what we want, or need, is easier than acknowledging what we have received. If you would build and maintain a strong positive self-image, develop an active sense of gratitude.

POINTER 10
Cultivate Strong Relationships!

Of course, everyone should be pleasant and easy to get along with in all contacts with people. Being well thought of usually comes as a result of treating people with dignity, respect, and consideration. However, the issue runs much deeper. A successful person may have thousands of acquaintances, but only a handful of friends.

True friends can do wonders for your self-esteem! "A friend is someone who knows all about you, and loves you anyway," someone has wisely said. Friends are those people Dr. Paul Tournier calls, "significant others." They really rejoice with you when you are happy, and they stick by you when the going is tough.

Life can crash in on us with brutal fury at times, and often at these times the only thing that can keep us going is knowing that someone really cares. Such friends may be members of your family or a few well-chosen companions, but in hours of deep anguish, they strangely resemble angels of mercy.

Like gratitude, friendships don't come automatically. They come as a result of giving ourselves to those we love. A wise old proverb says, "To have a friend, you must be a friend." No investment ever pays bigger dividends, over more years, than the investments you make in cultivating priceless companionships. Likewise, all your efforts to gain fame and fortune are ultimately worthless unless you have someone to share your victories with. Whatever else you do to build self-esteem, cultivate friendships.

A QUICK REVIEW

- Winners are made, not born. The primary difference between winners and losers is attitude. Winners make their goals, but losers make excuses.
- One of the most important parts of a winner's attitude is a strong positive self-image—a firm belief that you have value as a person, simply because you exist. As someone has said, "I am; therefore I matter!"
- Our self-image is the way we experience ourselves. When we experience ourselves positively, we have high self-esteem. To be successful and to enjoy the success you achieve, you must like yourself. You must believe at a very deep level that you are loved and lovable. And you must be willing to run the risk of loving others.

chapter six
I THINK I CAN,
I KNOW I CAN . . . I DID!

A woman came into my office one day and said, "Nido, someone told me you could help me. I've talked to many other people about my problem, and nobody's been able to help me," she continued.

"Well," I said warily, "What is this problem you think I can help with?"

"Everybody hates me," she said, "My husband hates me, my children hate me, the people where I work hate me . . . even my minister hates me!"

After listening to that woman for one hour, 22 minutes, and 17 seconds—*I hated her*!

Of course, I really didn't "hate" her, but I could understand why people found it hard to like her. She didn't give them much to like! Her low self-esteem reflected itself in the way she constantly put herself down. She exhibited an almost complete lack of self-confidence. If you are going to make life work for you, you must do two things:

- First, you must accept yourself as a valuable person created in the image of God. You gotta' like yourself!
- Second, you must sell yourself to other people! The place to start is to believe in yourself and your abilities—*to have self-confidence!*

SELF-CONFIDENCE

There are two sides to your personality: the way others affect you, and the way you affect others. The way you allow other people to affect you greatly influences your peace of mind, your personal happiness, and your ability to do important things. We talked a great deal about this point in the chapter on self-esteem. But did you realize that your success in life depends, in large measure, on the way you affect other people? "Nobody was ever very successful, unless a lot of other people wanted him (or her) to be successful," is an old and wise saying.

When we say someone is "effective," what do we mean? Usually, we mean that the person is able to get other people to do things. An effective salesperson can get people to buy. An effective minister can influence people to find meaning in life through a relationship with God. An effective supervisor can get people to accomplish the goals that management sets for them.

Yet personal effectiveness is more than being liked by others (although it usually includes that). It is more than the ability to order people around, and it is even more than the power to make people do what they don't want to do. I call effectiveness your "power to persuade" people to do things. It is your ability to sell yourself, your ideas, and your goals so effectively that others will want to assist you in achieving them. So how do you do that? The first step is to believe in yourself and in your abilities!

America's Greatest Athlete

When some forty top sports historians were asked to select the one person who stood out as the greatest athlete in the history of American sports, the almost unanimous choice was Babe Ruth. The historians felt he had made the best use of his talents, and his impact on his sport during his lifetime was very great. Asked what attribute made him so great, the sports authorities almost all pinpointed his self-confidence.

Nowhere is that belief in himself better illustrated than in the often repeated story of his most famous home run. In the pivotal game of the World Series, the Yankees were trailing. Quietly, "The Babe" stepped up to the plate in the last inning, with two outs and the bases loaded. A home run would win the game. The wildly cheering crowd reminded him that the world championship rested squarely on his shoulders.

"Strike one!" called the umpire. The crowd gasped and grew silent.

"Strike two!" came the next call. The Babe backed away from the plate, tightened his belt, adjusted his hat, and looked at the bat in his hand. Slowly, the old veteran stepped up to the plate. Casually, he lifted his left arm and pointed to the left field wall. The pitcher grinned. The crowd gasped with intensity!

There was a pitch, a swing, the solid crack of a bat, and slowly the ball rose. Up and up it went, right where The Babe had pointed—over the left field fence! The crowd went wild!

Later, in the locker room, a teammate asked the "Home Run King" how he would have felt if he had missed that ball after having pointed to the wall.

"Well, uh . . . it never crossed my mind," replied the old hero.

That's what self-confidence is all about—*believing you can do what you set out to accomplish!* A strong positive self-image says, "I have value as a person. I am somebody. I matter in this world!" Self-confidence says, "I am capable. I can cope with my environment. More than that—with the help of God—I can win at the game of life!"

Self-Confidence Is Not . . .

Perhaps some people back away from developing a strong sense of self-confidence because they have seen so many fakes.

Self-Confidence Is Not:
Bragging about your abilities and accomplishments
Putting down the abilities or accomplishments of others
Exaggerating your abilities or deeds
Out-talking everybody else to get your way

A better word for those practices is arrogance. Other words that come to mind are "conceit," "self-centeredness," "egotism." You can bet your bottom dollar that people who are always bragging, putting others down, exaggerating, or out-talking those around them are only trying to bolster their own sagging self-confidence.

"The Meek Shall Inherit . . ."

Real self-confidence tends to be quiet and soft-spoken. One of the sad quirks of the English language is that meekness rhymes with weakness. Thus all those poems that talk about the meekness of Jesus tend to center on that scene where He was a baby in a manger. We somehow have come to associate meekness with vulnerability, with being a milk toast, with a weakness in character.

The real definition of meekness is *controlled strength*. As the manhood of Jesus demonstrated, people who believe in themselves are more concerned with accomplishing their goals than they are with proving to everybody that they are great.

> *People Who Have Strong Self-Confidence Tend To:*
> Apply their personal power to useful goals
> Let others talk about their abilities and deeds
> Concentrate on goals, not activities
> Freely express admiration and appreciation to others

It is enough for them to know the value of their goals and to believe in their abilities to reach those goals. They are far more concerned that their actions speak louder than their words.

Maybe You're a Thoroughbred

"Created in the image of God" is pretty big billing! Measuring up to all that potential calls for the best you can do with all you've got. Maybe you've felt there was a touch of greatness in you. Maybe you've dared to hope you're a thoroughbred—that in your veins runs the blood of a champion.

Someone has said that there are actually two people inside each us: a big person who longs for greatness, and a little person who stands in the way and shouts, "You can't!"

For example, the famous tenor, Enrico Caruso, was waiting in the wings on opening night at the opera, and the house was packed. The great singer suddenly rasped in a loud whisper, "Get out of my way! Get out! Get out!" The stage hands were all baffled, because no one was even near him. They thought he was cracking up.

"I felt within the big me that wants to sing and knows it can, but it was being stifled by the little me that gets afraid and says I can't," the great singer later explained. "I was simply ordering that little me out of my body."

Self-doubt and fear of failure are the two great enemies of the real person that seeks to stand up inside each of us. They whittle away—if we let them—at the person we hope to become until we become timid and afraid to try. They sap our resources so that we can make use of only a small part of our mental capacities.

"The Music's Gone"

Self-confidence meets with resistance in many forms, but it always rises to the challenge. Ken Helser is an excellent musician who uses his talents very effectively in communicating with prisoners throughout the Southeast. "When I was a little boy," he often shares with the inmates, "I was given a little xylophone for Christmas. With it came a set of instructions. I was well on the way to learning how to play it when I lost the instruction booklet." After he and his parents had searched the house, the yard, and the family car, all to no avail, he sat down and began to cry.

"Mother," he had whined, "The music's gone!"

"No, son," his mother replied, "The instructions are gone . . . The music is inside you . . . listen to it, and you can play it."

"Here in prison," he tells the inmates, "you may feel cut off from everything, like life is closing in on you . . . like the music is gone from your life. But the music's inside you; if you listen to it, you can play it!"

Wherever you are, whatever your circumstances may be, whatever misfortune you may have suffered, the music of your life has not gone. It's inside you—if you listen to it, you can play it. "Little minds are tamed and subdued by misfortunes, but great minds rise above them," said Washington Irving. Emerson said it this way; "He is great who is great from nature, and who reminds us of no one else."

The people with self-confidence are cheerful when it's difficult to be cheerful, patient when it's difficult to be patient. They push ahead when they want to stand still. They keep trying long after the circumstances, and perhaps other people, say they are beaten.

Self-Confidence Plus Struggle Equals Character

Once a little girl watched a moth trying to struggle free from its cocoon. Seeking to help the beautiful creature, she reached into her pocket and pulled out her knife. Ever-so-carefully, she cut away the cocoon and freed the moth. For a long time, she watched the moth as it flapped its wings and tried unsuccessfully to fly. Finally, the wings sagged for the last time, and the moth died. "Sis," her older sister later explained, "The struggle gives strength to the moth's wings. When you cut away the cocoon, you took away the very exercise that would have enabled it to fly."

Of course, none of us likes to struggle with difficulties and misfortunes, but wise persons accept them as opportunities to grow. Wise and self-confident persons welcome the struggle—the resistance—because they know it is the best way to develop character. In fact, such persons understand that troubles build personal courage and magnanimity. If learning were easy, our mental powers would never be developed. If work were not necessary and we never exercised physically, our bodies would never grow in strength. If everything in life were a "bed of roses," we would never develop character beyond that of a child.

SELF-DISCIPLINE, THE MASTER KEY

The master key to self-confidence is self-discipline. Self-confidence is the ability to bring to bear the full resources of our minds, our bodies, and our spirits to cope with whatever challenge lies before us. That can happen only when we are under complete self-control. Thomas Huxley wrote:

> That man, I think, has a liberal education whose body has been so trained in youth that it is the ready servant of his will, and does with ease and pleasure all that, as a mechanism, it is capable of; whose intellect is a clear, cold, logic engine, with all its parts of equal strength and in smooth running order, ready, like a steam engine, to be turned to any kind of work and to spin the gossamers as well as forge the anchors of the mind; whose mind is stored with the knowledge of the great fundamental truths of nature and the laws of her operations; one who is full of life and fire; but whose passions have been trained to come to heel by a vigorous will, the servant of a tender conscience, one who has learned to love all beauty, whether of nature or of art, to hate all vileness, and to esteem others as himself.

As the great Caruso was able to order the little person within him to "get out of the way," each of us can take charge of the self-doubts that seek to keep us from realizing our full potential. We don't have to wait for permission from the negative self that struggles for our attention. We can go ahead and act in self-confidence.

"If it feels good, do it!" is the credo of many of today's youth. But the person who wants to build self-confidence operates on the belief that, "If you keep doing what is right, it will begin to feel good."

You Can, If You Believe You Can

Researchers at a leading university selected a large group of athletes for an experiment. The athletes were told that they were going to be asked to do some exercises that no one had ever been able to do. The researchers told them that, since they were among the best athletes in the country, they would be able to do the exercises.

The athletes were divided into two groups, and the first group was taken to the gymnasium. Try as they might, they couldn't quite do the exercises.

The second group was then led to the gym and told of the failure of the first group.

"But, you will be different," the researchers said. "Take this little pill. This new drug enables you to function at a superhuman level."

Surely enough, the second group of athletes went out and did the exercises quite easily.

"What kind of pill was that?" one of the participants asked.

"It contained nothing more than chalk," was the reply.

The second group was able to accomplish the impossible—because they believed they could! If you believe you can—and believe it strongly enough—you will be amazed at what you can do.

SELF-CONFIDENCE CAN MAKE
THE DIFFERENCE

I can promise you that, if you set out to do anything worthwhile, plenty of small-minded people will tell you it can't be done. At times, you may feel as though you are the only person alive who believes in your ability to do something. But don't let your doubts and the doubts of others stop you! Your self-confidence can make the difference in success and failure.

The next chapter offers ten tested and proven steps toward building a strong sense of self-confidence. They have worked well for me, and I believe they will work for you.

chapter seven
TEN STEPS
TO BUILDING
SELF-CONFIDENCE

"What lies behind us and what lies before us are tiny matters compared to what lies within us," said Emerson.

Occasionally, the news media carry stories of people who have demonstrated superhuman capacity in some emergency. Recently they told of such an amazing feat by a 12-year-old boy. The boy's father was working under a truck, which weighed about 3,000 pounds, when the jack gave way and the truck fell. Seeing his father being squeezed to death, the boy seized the truck's bumper and lifted the vehicle high enough to allow his father to slide from beneath it. The next day, the youngster could not budge the heavy truck.

Few of us have had that kind of dramatic experience. Yet most of us have had moments when we were amazed at what we have been able to do under certain circumstances.

Wouldn't it be great if we could operate at peak capacity at all times? Perhaps that's too much to ask—especially since scientists tell us that the greatest geniuses have succeeded only in using about 10 percent of their brains' capacity. But one thing seems clear: *All of us could consistently perform at a higher level than we normally do, if we had greater self-confidence.*

Here are ten steps by which you can build self-confidence. They will work effectively no matter what your present level of self-confidence. As these steps become cultivated habits of your daily life, they can enable you to face every challenge with a deeper confidence in yourself and in your abilities.

STEP 1
Decide What Limitations
You Will Accept

Two common errors can devastate your sense of self-confidence.

- First, it is a mistake to assume that all limits are self-imposed.
- Second, it is equally foolish and self-defeating to knuckle under to self-imposed limits.

Building self-confidence involves choosing which limitations you will accept, and which you will resist.

> *God grant me the serenity to accept the things I cannot change;*
> *The courage to change the things I can change;*
> *And the wisdom to know the difference.*

That old prayer has helped more people sort out where they should place the thrust of their efforts and concerns than any of us can imagine.

Some Limitations Are Real. Neal Austin has had a long and distinguished career as a librarian and a leader in the library field. Also a widely acclaimed author, he has written several biographies of literary figures. Yet, Neal was born with seriously deformed hands.

"Son," his father told him at an early age, "you will never be able to make a living with your hands, so you'd better develop your brain." Neal took his father's advice, and the world is a better place because he didn't sit around complaining about how unfortunate he was. He accepted his limitations and channeled his energies into developing his strengths.

People who beat themselves furiously against their natural limitations tend to become frustrated and embittered. They hold unrealistic ideals to which they try to measure up, often becoming "square pegs in round holes." They robbed the world of what they could do best because they spend their lives trying to do what they can do only poorly or not at all. Constant failure beats them down, and they lose all semblance of self-confidence. Such people expend all their energies chasing what is really an "impossible dream."

Of course, "The Impossible Dream" is a great and inspiring title for a song, but it is a lousy way to spend your life. I prefer the concept of "practical dreaming," that is, dreaming *possible* dreams about what you do best. Usually the first step in determining what you can do best is ruling out what you can do only poorly or not at all. Then you are free to concentrate all of your creative energies on your abilities and strengths.

Most Limitations Are Self-Imposed. An Eastern bishop was accustomed to paying an annual visit to a small religious college. On one such visit, the bishop engaged in an after-dinner conversation with the college president. The religious leader offered the opinion that the millenium could not be long in coming since everything about nature had been discovered, and all possible inventions had been made. The college president disagreed, stating that he felt the next fifty years would bring amazing discoveries and inventions. In his opinion, human beings would be flying through the skies like the birds within a relatively short time.

"Nonsense!" shouted the bishop. "Flight is reserved for the angels!"

The bishop's name was Wright. He had two sons—Orville and Wilbur.

The stories of most of the truly great achievements of history can almost always start with the words, "They said it couldn't be done!" For example, the consensus of athletes, coaches, doctors, and other sports experts for many years was that nobody would ever be able to run the mile in less than four minutes. That was before a young man named Roger Bannister did it in 1954. Since then, many runners have done the mile in less than four minutes.

The opinions of others or your own self-doubts can often stifle your belief in your abilities and in the possibility of a project. Self-confidence is often little more than a feeling, way down in the pit of your stomach, that you can do something that reason says is impossible. But, as you respond positively to that little feeling, it grows and grows until it reaches full bloom in concrete action.

The Secret Is in the Choice. The secret to taking this step is in making the right choice as to what limits you will accept and as to what limits you refuse to be bound by. At first, those choices might be a little hard to make. You might even have to fail sometimes to find out how to choose more effectively. But that's okay! It's better to try to do something and fail than to try nothing and succeed! As you try more and more, you can learn more about your strengths and limitations. And the choices become easier and more natural.

Keep this in mind: The "big self" inside you is always in a better position to know what you can or cannot do. As you respond positively to that inner person who longs to control your life, you will find that self-confidence grows up automatically.

STEP 2

Focus Attention on Your Greatest Strengths

Great achievers have learned the secret of concentrated energy. They have gotten in touch with their inner resources and discovered what they can do best—what they think is worth giving their best to accomplish. And they have learned to channel all their energies into a single purpose. "Always lead with your strong suit" is good advice.

Winners are like rivers. They find—or make—a deep channel and follow its course from where they are to where they want to go. Stand beside a great river sometime and think about how powerful it is. It can generate electricity, move terrain, and provide a setting for great wealth. Why? It concentrates all its movement in one direction!

Losers are more like swamps. They just spread out all over the place. They tend to try a little bit of everything, and really succeed at nothing. If you find yourself standing beside a swamp someday, watch what comes from it. Throughout the swamp you'll find bogs that mire people down, mosquitoes that are good for nothing but sucking blood and carrying diseases, alligators and all kinds of venomous snakes that can harm humans.

As you learn to concentrate on your strengths, and on what you can do well, you will feel your self-confidence rising up within you. For example, sportscasters generally agree that the thing that made Muhammed Ali practically unbeatable during his prime was that he always made his opponent "fight his fight." He would "float like a butterfly and sting like a bee." Beneath the poetry and self-adoration lay a great fighter who knew what he could do best and stuck to it. No wonder he made many far more powerful fighters believe he was "The Greatest."

One problem most of us face is that we can do so many things reasonably well. Abraham Lincoln would have made an excellent trial lawyer, but he chose to be a statesman. He had a deep sense of being placed on this earth to make a specific contribution at a critical point in our history. Hence, he determined with everything within himself to keep his rendezvous with destiny.

J. B. Phillips, the great Greek scholar and Bible translator, gives an interesting rendition of the idea expressed in the book of Romans. He says, "Don't let the world around you squeeze you into its own mold, but let God remold your mind from within. . . ." Isn't that a graphic picture of what happens to some of the most talented and capable people in the world. They get squeezed into a mold that shapes their lives to fit their circumstances or the images of other people. The sad thing is that the world is robbed of the real contributions they could make.

To build self-confidence, make the world fight your fight—get in touch with what you can do best and what you want most to do. Then spend your life doing it. The better you become at it, the more self-confidence you build.

STEP 3

Cultivate the Faith Within You

Learn to be kind to yourself. Keep a list of your triumphs and successes. As you focus on what you have done, you will have more confidence in what you can do. Only the loser's mentality causes one to focus on weaknesses and failures.

Most of us have demonstrated more self-confidence than we realize. Belief in yourself started when you were small. You believed you could walk before you took your first step. You believed you could talk before you said your first word. And you believed you could do worthwhile work before you took your first job. As you have believed, so have you achieved.

My favorite definition of "believing" is "accepting as true." The positive outgrowth of that is that we act as if something is true. When we act as if we accept our abilities, we find that they are real.

It really works! For example, the night before Douglas MacArthur took his entrance exam for West Point, he was all nerves. "Doug," his mother said to him, "you'll win if you don't lose your nerve. You must believe in yourself, my son, or no one else will believe in you. Be self-confident, self-reliant, and even if you don't make it, you will know you have done your best." When the test scores were announced, Douglas MacArthur was number one on the list.

Make it a habit to act as if the best things you hope about your abilities are true. You will not only find that you have more self-confidence, but you'll also find that your self-confidence is justified by your performance. Remember that little song from "The King And I?"

> *Whenever I feel afraid, I hold my head erect,*
> *And whistle a happy tune, so no one will suspect*
> *I'm afraid.*

> *The result of this deception is very clear to tell;*
> *For when I fool the people I'm with,*
> *I fool myself as well.*

Make cultivating faith in yourself a daily—even a moment-by-moment—exercise, and you can build your self-confidence.

STEP 4
Prepare Yourself to Be the Best

A young man named Demosthenes, by asking to speak to the leaders of ancient Athens, stepped into a spot that some of the greatest orators of history had occupied. His voice was weak and faltering, his manner timid, and his thoughts muddled. Also, he spoke with a stammer. When he had finished, the crowd booed and hissed him off the platform.

But Demosthenes was not to be held down.

"Never again will I speak unprepared!" he promised himself. And prepare he did! He cultivated his voice by shouting to the top of his lungs into the Aegean Sea. He practiced his speeches under a dangling sword to bolster his courage. He practiced for hours on end with pebbles in his mouth to eliminate his stammer. He prepared his speeches so well that he was accused of over preparing them.

The next time he addressed the assembly, he was a different man. With eloquent words, powerful voice, and stately manner, he drew uproarious cheers from his audience. When he had finished, the crowd arose as one person and shouted, "Let us go and fight Phillip!"

How could a faltering, stammering, stage-frightened young man rise from rejection and failure to become the greatest orator of Greek history? The answer involves one word—preparation! Demosthenes knew that his first speech did not represent the best that he could do. He was able to overcome his self-doubts and stage-fright only by preparing himself to be the best he could be at what he had set out to do.

If you want the kind of self-confidence that enables you to perform to the upper limits of your ability, you can have it only when you prepare adequately. Then, and only then, can you step confidently into the arena of your life and face your competitors with courage and excitement.

Even when you get past the rudiments of your job, mastering the basic techniques of doing your task, you are ready to move on to the arduous preparation required to become a master. The story is told of an old master of the piano who was able to move people to tears with her music. "How often do you practice?" she was asked by an aspiring young musician.

"Six hours everyday!" replied the old master.

"But, madam," protested her young protege, "you have been playing for so long, and you are so good . . ."

"I wish to be superb," replied the wise old woman.

Self-confidence is the slight edge that usually lifts the winner above the "also-rans." The belief in your abilities comes only from preparation.

STEP 5
Cultivate Friends Who Believe in You

What you say to yourself is most important; we tend to live up to our own expectations of ourselves. But what those around you say about your abilities can have a great deal of impact on your self-confidence; because we also try to live up to the expectations of those around us. Tell children all their lives that they are stupid, and they grow up to believe it. Expect great things of them, and they are likely to achieve great things.

Have you noticed that some people sap your self-confidence and leave you with feelings of self-doubt? Yet, you draw strength from others who build your self-confidence. It is sometimes surprising to notice that the people who sap your belief in yourself are not the truly great people around you. They are the small-minded individuals who are always complaining. Generally, those who might have reason to belittle your abilities are the most apt to encourage you to try. For example, my humorist friend, Joe Larson, told me once, "My friends didn't believe that I can become a successful speaker. So, I did something about it. I went out and found me some new friends!"

Some of the greatest success stories of history have followed a word of encouragement or an act of confidence by a loved one or a trusting friend. Had it not been for a confident wife, Sophia, we might not have listed among the great names of literature the name of Nathanial Hawthorne. When Nathaniel, a heart-broken man, went home to tell his wife that he had been fired from his job in a customhouse and confess that he was a failure, she surprised him with a exclamation of joy.

"Now," she said triumphantly, "you can write your book!"

"Yes," replied the man, with sagging confidence, "and what shall we live on while I am writing it?"

To his amazement, she opened a drawer and pulled out a substantial amount of money.

"Where on earth did you get that?" he exclaimed.

"I have always known that you were a man of genius," she answered, "I knew that someday you would write a masterpiece. So every week, out of the money you have given me for housekeeping, I have saved something; here is enough to last us for one whole year."

From her trust and confidence came one of the greatest novels of American literature, *The Scarlet Letter*.

Cultivate relationships with people who bolster your self-confidence, who expect the best from you, and who urge you to become all that you can be. Sometimes you'll find such people among the pages of great books. The late President John F. Kennedy regularly studied what the great people of history did, and he patterned his life after their "habits of leadership and greatness."

Building self-confidence is one of the few games in life that everybody can win. In other words, you can reverse the process by building up other people's self-confidence and inspire them to reach their true greatness. Your self-confidence will benefit greatly from receiving and giving the strokes of encouragement that come from mutually supportive relationships.

STEP 6
Learn from Your Mistakes and Failures: Don't Let them Defeat You

The only way you can avoid making mistakes is to make the biggest mistake of all—do nothing. Some mistakes truly hold serious consequences—sometimes far out of proportion to the "ease" with which they are made. However, no failure, misfortune, or mistake is ever so great that nothing good can come from it.

The wise person always seeks to learn something of value from each mistake or failure. The loser gains nothing from trying and coming up short.

"I've been here twenty years," complained an employee who had just been bypassed for a promotion. "I've got twenty years of experience over the person you just promoted!"

"No, Charlie," said his boss, "you've had one year of experience twenty times. You haven't learned from the mistakes you have made. You're still making the same mistakes you made during your first year here."

What a sad story! Even if a mistake seems trivial, don't compound it by failing to learn something of value from it.

"We've wasted so much time!" shouted a young assistant to Thomas Edison. "We've tried twenty-thousand tests, and we still haven't found a material that works as a filament!"

"Ah!" responded the genius. "But we now know twenty-thousand things that won't work!"

This indomitable spirit enabled Edison to eventually find a filament that would produce light—and change the course of history.

An important step in building your self-confidence is learning to hold your mistakes and failures in proper perspective. The key lies in tying your sense of personal security to something deeper than immediate success. You can build and maintain your self-confidence by balancing your failures and mistakes against your long-term goals, your underlying purpose in life, and your inherent worth as a human being—rather than against their immediate consequences. No mistake you could ever make would strip you of your value as a human being. Most mistakes detour you only slightly on your road to fulfilling your purpose in life. Mistakes are seldom fatal. More often, the person's attitude toward them is fatal or at least seriously damaging. Persons who can come out of each mistake or failure better equipped to face the future are not only able to salvage self-confidence, but they are also able to build it ever stronger.

STEP 7
Learn to Accept Constructive Criticism and to Ignore Petty Criticism

"My teacher doesn't like me!" the little girl said to her father.

"Why do you say that?" asked the father.

"She gave me an 'F' on this paper," came the quick answer, "and just look at all these red marks all over it!"

"I think she must like you a lot," said the father after reading the paper. "She knows that you are capable of far better writing than this. And she even went to the trouble to show you how to improve it!"

Nobody likes to be criticised! Even when we have not done our best—and we know it—it hurts to hear someone we love say they know we could have done better. Yet our real friends are the ones who won't let us get away with sloppy work or half-hearted efforts. Gently, ever so gently, they tell us that they expected better from us. These criticisms, in their own way, are actually compliments. Learning to graciously accept constructive criticism not only can improve our performance, but it can also help us build self-confidence by seeing that we can do better.

The "cheap shots" from the envious, the insecure, or the negative are another matter entirely. The more successful you become, and the better you become at what you do, the more of these grumblers you will attract. Such criticism is best ignored! It usually does nothing to improve your performance, and it always tears at your self-confidence. Learn something from it if you can. Otherwise, forget it and move on.

STEP 8
Celebrate Your Victories

When you have done your very best or have done something well, patting yourself on the back is not egotistic. In fact, it can be a great builder of self-confidence.

Even when someone else signs your paycheck, you are working for yourself. Learn to be kind to your most valuable employee—yourself! An employee once said that her boss was very generous with vacations, with periodic raises, and with fringe benefits. He always provided a comfortable work environment. "But I'd trade it all for one simple acknowledgement that I had done a good job," she said.

To build self-confidence, reward yourself for your efforts and accomplishments, and celebrate your victories.

STEP 9
Cultivate a Sense of Humility

People who become arrogant and overly proud of themselves somehow, sooner or later, get knocked down by failure. Many people can take misfortune in stride and keep going, but they are spoiled by success. They tend to forget where they have come from and to look down their noses at those they feel are beneath them.

An interesting thing happens to people who fall into that trap. They tend to become paranoid about the intentions of everyone around them, cutting themselves off from those whom they desperately need. The next step is often severe doubts about their own abilities to maintain the level of performance they have set for themselves. You might find them trying to bolster their self-confidence by cutting down those they see as competitors, or by trying to maintain their lofty perch by tearing others down.

It is a mark of insecurity—not self-confidence—to always be

talking about your abilities and accomplishments. Holding your abilities and deeds in perspective is not only important in maintaining friendships, it goes a long way toward building self-confidence. "Really great persons," said John Ruskin, "have the feeling that the greatness is not in them but through them." Sir Francis Bacon wrote, "The less people speak of their greatness, the more we think of it."

New challenges are important, but they should be the challenges we choose, rather than the challenges forced on us by trying to live up to an image we have established. For example, one of the classic plots of the old western movies is that of a gunfighter who has built up such a reputation that all challengers are out to "outdraw" him to bolster their own reputations. Sooner or later, the gunfighter is overtaken by his own record.

Freely admitting a mistake is another element of true humility. When you readily admit that you are capable of making mistakes, and that you do make mistakes, they are not so devastating to your self-confidence when they do occur. "Eating crow" is never pleasant—no matter how much mustard and ketchup you put on it. But usually the sooner you eat it, the less unpleasant it is to the taste!

If you would build self-confidence, cultivate a sense of true humility.

STEP 10
Keep Expanding Your Horizons

Without new challenges we develop what someone has called "hardening of the attitudes." Only when your memories are more important to you than your goals are you old. For example, I have long admired the indomitable spirit of George Burns. Here is a man who, by every human measure, has been very successful. He has had several careers, and he has set a tremendous pace for others to follow in each of them. Now, despite advancing age, he refuses to stop reaching out to take on new projects.

Dr. Norman Vincent Peale is another one of those great spirits who cannot be stopped by age and who refuses to live in the past. He is still writing books, giving those inspiring talks, and counseling with people who need to discover "The Power of Positive

Thinking!" Dr. Peale is the best evidence I know of his claim that "Enthusiasm Makes the Difference." Here is a person whose self-confidence has continued to grow, because he has kept reaching out.

People who live on past glories, and who fail to keep their self-confidence growing, find that they gradually lose the faith they once had in their abilities. Slowly, they begin to talk more and more about "the good old days," and less and less about the wonderful years that lie ahead. I'm sure you've seen those movies that portray the impact of living in the past: scenes of an old actor displaying reviews from by-gone plays, a punchdrunk fighter telling a kid how good he "used to be," or an aging athlete looking through blurred eyes at trophies from ancient victories

You don't have to be a senior citizen for this to happen to you. Recently, a young man—in his early thirties—told me that since he had reached the lifetime goal he had set for himself, he was becoming bored with life. Terms like "burnout," "mid-life crisis," and "early retirement" are becoming more and more common in analyses of what is wrong with our national mental health. One of the best prescriptions for self-confidence I have ever heard is the old saying, "Keep learning, earning, and yearning."

Faith in our abilities is shored up by a sense of purpose, by an awareness of meaning, and by a feeling that we are contributing something worthwhile to the world around us. Those things are ours only when we are reaching out to new horizons.

LOOKING BACK AND AHEAD

By consistently practicing these ten steps we can increase our effectiveness at whatever we choose to do.

To get a clearer idea of how to keep reaching out, let's take a look at the next chapter: "Goals: The Way You Control Your Life."

chapter eight
GOALS: THE WAY
YOU CONTROL
YOUR LIFE

You can take charge of your life in only one way: through setting and living your life by goals. One thing about really successful people is that *they seem to know where they are going*. They have learned to set goals for themselves, and they expend all of their creative energy pursuing those goals.

Do you remember, for example, the scene from *Alice in Wonderland*, in which Alice met the Cheshire Cat? Several roads lay before her, and she was having a hard time choosing which to travel.

"Which way should I go?" she asked the Cheshire Cat.

"Where do you wish to go?" replied the cat.

"Oh! It really doesn't matter," answered Alice.

"Then, it really doesn't make any difference which way you go," grinned the Cheshire Cat.

Many unsuccessful people are extremely busy—*they are always doing something*. However, what they are doing cannot take them anywhere because they don't know where they want to go. They fall victim to circumstances. They feel pressured by other people into doing things they don't really want to do. And they remain frustrated because they always seem to be going in circles.

For example, consider this conversation between a young woman and a counsellor:

"You feel that to get what you want out of life you'll have to get a master's degree?" asked the counsellor.

"Yes," said the young woman, "but by the time I could get

that degree, I'd be thirty years old! I can't afford to wait that long to get started in a career."

"But won't you be thirty years old, even without the degree?" asked the counsellor.

The counsellor's prediction proved accurate. At age thirty, the woman was without her degree, mired down in a job she hated, with little hope of going back to school. She had focused all of her attention on her circumstances, instead of on her longterm goals. This tendency is a mark of the immaturity that is so typical of today's youth.

Consider the progression of a teenager I talked with recently:

> He bought a car so he could have transportation.
> He got a job so he could pay for the car.
> He dropped out of high school, so he could get a better job,
> And buy a newer car.

This is the age of "instant everything." Clever writers and producers can solve the most complicated dilemmas within thirty minutes, or an hour at the most, in a television drama. We can get instant relief from acid indigestion by knowing how to spell a certain word, bedazzle a prospective mate by using a certain toothpaste, and handle a tough new job by wearing a certain kind of deodorant.

But most of the things that make life worth living require time to develop. They don't come about quickly or easily. Furthermore, they don't happen automatically. The practical dreamers know the harder they work, the luckier they get.

They Know That:
Careers take time and energy to build.
  Lasting relationships require tremendous personal investments.
    Financial security usually has to be built up over many years.

If you will learn to set realistic and worthwhile goals for every area of your life, and pursue those goals with everything within you, you can become one of life's real winners.

HOW TO SET AND MONITOR GOALS

How do you set and monitor your goals? Here are seven guidelines that represent the collective experience of many of the most successful people in America. They have been tested and proven in the laboratory of life. I have found, in my own life, that they work.

GUIDELINE 1
Identify Your Purpose in Life

Close your eyes for eyes for a moment and try to imagine what you would like for your life to be like ten years from now. Keep in mind that you are a total person. Setting financial goals to meet your needs and desires in life is important. Somebody once said that, "Whether you are rich or poor, it's always nice to have money." But there's more to life than just making money. Perhaps you read the story in recent newspapers about a California girl who received a very special birthday cake on her twenty-first birthday. Around each of the twenty-one candles was wrapped a thousand-dollar bill. A few days later, her parents found the body of that young lady. In her hand was a suicide note that said, "You have given me everything to live with, but nothing to live for!" What a tragedy!

In choosing your purpose in life, you have to answer three big questions:

1. *Who am I?* A simple exercise can help you focus on this question. Write a short essay telling who you are—but with the following limitations: Eliminate your name, age, educational background, address, biographical information, or any of the other things you would normally include on a resume. The only question that really matters is, "Who are you as a person?"
2. *What am I doing here?* What do you wish to contribute, with your life, that will both enrich you as a person and make the world a better place in which to live? Write an epitaph for yourself. Reduce to a few words what you would like for people to say about you, after you have departed this life.
3. *Where am I going?* In light of the preceding two exercises, reduce to one short sentence what direction you will pursue with your life. Now rate yourself, on a scale of 1 to 10, as to how your performance in life to date has measured up to the purpose you have identified.

Figure 8 –1. Ten Good Reasons For Setting Goals

Setting and diligently working toward goals can help you take charge of your life for ten good reasons:

1. Goals give you something to work for—purpose and direction to your life.
2. Goals give you the best reason in the world for not procrastinating.
3. Goals help you to concentrate all your energies and resources in the specific direction you have chosen.
4. Goals help you to build enthusiasm.
5. Goals help you to be specific with other people who would like to help you.
6. Goals help you to save time for yourself, for the people for whom you work, and for everyone else in your life.
7. Goals help you to make and save money.
8. Goals help you to keep in perspective what really matters.
9. Goals give you a standard against which to measure your effectiveness as a person.
10. Goals provide a foundation for setting new goals—they help you to keep reaching out.

As you identify your purpose in life, remember that your life has many dimensions. It is important to choose:

1. a career that not only offers financial rewards, but that satisfies your deep needs for satisfaction and meaning;
2. personal and family relationships that bring love to your life;
3. community and religious goals that satisfy your spiritual and altruistic needs; and
4. cultural and recreational goals that enrich your life and make it fun to live.

GUIDELINE 2
Choose Goals That Are
Consistent with the Way You See Yourself

Choose those goals that will enable you to become the person you want to become. Allow room for growth, for reaching out, for reaching up. Let's review briefly the three steps toward building a winner's attitude, as outlined in Chapter 3:

1. Make a strong and permanent commitment to invest your life and talents only in those pursuits that deserve your best efforts.
2. Make a strong and irrevocable commitment to give all that you have, and all that you are, to achieve the goals you have set for yourself.
3. Make a strong commitment to reach your full potential as a human being.

With these steps in mind, select the goals that will take you into the winner's circle of life.

People might not understand, or agree with the choices you make, but you are the person you must please. "You cannot consistently perform in a manner that is inconsistent with the way you see yourself," someone has wisely pointed out. For example, Albert Schweitzer gave up a prestigious career as a doctor and went to Africa to build hospitals for the poor and ignorant natives. Many of his friends, who felt that he was throwing away his talents and training, sent a delegation to Africa to attempt to persuade him to come back to his native land.

"Why should such a gifted man give up so much to labor among the savages?" they asked.

"Don't talk about sacrifice," Schweitzer replied, "What does it matter where one goes provided one can do good work there? Much as I appreciate your kind words and thoughts, I have made up my mind to stay in Africa and look after my African friends."

In Africa he remained until he died in 1965, at the age of 90. He worked until the very end, maintaining his zest for living. His whole life was a powerful message. His philosophy was: "The only essential thing is to seek truth, and to practice it as far as we understand it." This great man had a clear vision of himself. He knew what was important to him, and he devoted his life to pursuing it.

The person who matters most is the one who stares back at you from the mirror. If your goals, and the commitment you make to them, permit you to look upon yourself with self-respect, and to maintain your feeling that life is worthwhile, what does it really matter what anyone else thinks? After all, choosing the goals on which you will spend the days allotted to you is what taking charge of your life is all about. Literature and history are full of stories about people who allowed the opinions of others to dominate their lives, only to be disappointed with what they turned out to be.

"Know thyself" is good advice that has been passed down through the ages. As you constantly attempt to stay in touch with the deep values that have become a part of your life, and act in a manner that is consistent with those values, you can find peace of mind, happiness, and success in life.

GUIDELINE 3
Write Down Your Goals and Set
Definite Timetables for Reaching Them

Your goals should be both believable and achievable. Setting realistic goals permits self-satisfaction and a sense of accomplishment to be a normal part of your everyday life. You'll find that you feel better about yourself, and less tired, as you reach those achievable goals.

Get very definite with your goals. If you set about to do something in a general way, that's usually the way you will do it. Be specific; be concrete. Precisely what do you want to accomplish?

Three types of goals are desirable:

1. *Long-Range Goals*: These are things you want to accomplish either during your lifetime or in a five- or ten-year period. It helps to know where you ultimately want to go.
2. *Intermediate Goals*: Break your long-range goals down into more short-term goals. These would include things you want to do during the next year or six months. Always balance your intermediate goals against your long-range goals.
3. *Short-Range Goals*: Further break down your long- and intermediate range goals into monthly and weekly goals that move you toward your target.

"The palest ink is more enduring than the strongest memory," says an old oriental proverb. In the mad pace of daily living, it is easy to loose sight of your goals. Therefore, it is a great aid to have them written out and easily accessible. Many people have found it helpful to write their goals in the form of a contract with themselves; with definite dates set for the fulfillment of specific increments. It is a great idea!

GUIDELINE 4
Break Your Goals Down
Into Easily Achievable Objectives

Dr. Robert Schuller constantly reminds us that, "Yard by yard, life is hard; but inch by inch it's a cinch." I like that! I've found it to be quite true. "A journey of a thousand miles begins with a single step," is another bit of ancient oriental philosophy that makes this point. As long as your goals are far-distant hopes and dreams, they are not likely to begin happening. But once you start breaking them down into manageable steps, they can become real to you.

For example, let's say you have chosen to increase your effectiveness by reading at least 36 books during the next year. That might sound like an "impossible dream." But if you break the goal down into a series of objectives, you can easily read three books per month. If you do so every month, you will have read 36 books in one year.

The principle is the same for each of your goals. Put each goal into a manageable objective. Even an otherwise boring job can take on new meaning if you see it as a part of the necessary work to accomplish your long-term goals. You can get excited about even mundane tasks—provided they are taking you somewhere you have chosen to go. As long as you are doing something every day to lead you toward your goals, you can hold life's bumps and scrapes in the proper perspective.

Someone asked an old man how he could remain so cheerful in the midst of so many calamities. "I've read the Bible all the way through; and I've noticed that it often says, 'It came to pass.' Nowhere does it say that it came to stay." What an outlook!

The key question for each activity you are considering is not "What will it do for me?" but "How will it help me reach my goal?" If most of the things you are doing do not move you toward your goals, your time is being eroded away—a minute at a time.

Urgent Versus Important

The big game most of us tend to play with our daily lives is choosing how we will expend our precious minutes and creative energies. Urgencies forever seem to eat up hours at a time. Unfortunately, many of the things that seem so urgent to us at the moment are not really that important in the total picture of our lives. For example, a friend shared with me recently that he had been so busy taking care of urgent things during the last twenty years that he had not noticed that his children had suddenly grown up. "I just looked around one day, and they were gone," he said. Interestingly, that man couldn't remember most of the things that had robbed him of those precious moments he could have spent cultivating his relationship with his children.

When we invest our lives in responding to urgencies, we allow circumstances and other people to choose for us how we will live. The only cure for wasting our lives "putting out brush fires" is to have a specific and clearly focused objective that we should be working on at any given moment. When we know what objective will move us closer to our goals, then we can weigh the urgency against what is really important to us in the long run.

GUIDELINE 5
Make Your Dreams Come True

Once you have decided what you want to do with your life, and the steps you must take to make it happen, *do it*! Learn to discipline yourself to work toward the priorities that you have set. Your boss will set quotas and targets for you to reach. Your family will constantly remind you of their needs and desires. And you can be sure that the Internal Revenue Service will demand its regular payments from you. However, *only you can place the demands on yourself that are necessary to meet your goals*.

The value in any decision is in its implementation. At this point, most goals break down. Ask most people to tell you on the first of July how many of their New Year's resolutions they have kept, and they will confess that they can't even remember what they were. You can't spend money you were "going to make someday." You can't enjoy books you only "intended to read." And you can't live on memories of ideas you once had.

Of course, it's important to be flexible enough to adjust your goals to take advantage of new opportunities and situations. For example, a young man in my hometown of High Point, North Carolina, had set a goal of winning a Gold Medal in the Olympics.

For years, he ran ten miles every morning before going to school, he read everything he could find about running, and he sought out the best coaches to guide him in his development. He was well on his way to becoming an Olympic class runner, when his right leg was seriously injured in an automobile wreck. The injury was so permanently crippling that he knew he'd never be able to run again. He was heart-broken!

But this was a remarkable young man. After a few days of grieving over his loss, he decided to become a coach for other runners. Now he's training three boys and two girls to become contenders. Certainly, he's disappointed at not making his primary goal, but he has learned the secret of redirection. In other words, "If life gives you lemons, make yourself a big glass of lemonade."

I have noticed that people who concentrate all their energies on reaching their goals not only are more apt to accomplish something worthwhile with their lives, but they can shift their priorities to adjust to new situations more comfortably than people who just wander aimlessly through life. "Your attitude, not your aptitude, will determine your altitude," is a wise and often repeated saying. Nowhere is attitude more important than in pursuing your goals.

Taking charge of your life means that you decide what you want to do, and do it!

GUIDELINE 6
Review Your Goals Often and Check Your Progress

It is a good idea to evaluate your effectiveness on the basis of how close you come to attaining your goals. How busy you have been is not nearly so important as how many of your goals you have reached. Many very successful people set definite appointments with themselves for a time of review. They write down the time they set, and, they refuse to allow anything to conflict with their date with themselves.

As you review your goals, if you find that you have missed a deadline, find out why you have missed it. Formulate a contingency plan for meeting it at a later date, and renew your commitment to that goal. Also, reward yourself for each goal you reach. Doing so renews your self-confidence and gives you added incentive to keep pressing on toward all your other goals.

Just as you would not write a check without noting the amount of money you are spending, don't allow those precious moments to slip away unnoticed. Make a regular practice of balancing your "goal account" just as you balance your checking account. If you find that someone, or some activity, is making unauthorized withdrawals from your deposits of time, put a stop to it.

GUIDELINE 7
Constantly Set New Goals

A man constantly complained that he could never get caught up. Every day for twenty years he looked at the stack of unfinished tasks on his desk. There were always bills to pay, letters to answer, appointments that had to be met, and problems to be solved. When he went home to get away from the clutter of demands, he found a yard to be cut, hedges to be trimmed, and repairs to be made. Just once, he'd like to get caught up, he thought.

In the midst of his struggle, he fell asleep and had a dream. He was in a large office with a beautiful modern desk. On it there were no appointments, no papers, no bills—nothing to do. So he went home. There he found the lawn neatly cut, the hedges all trimmed, and all the repairs completed. It was a great relief. He had caught up at last.

Exercise 8–1. Seven Guidelines

A. If you already have formulated a set of goals, and put them in operation, evaluate them in light of the Seven Guidelines. Rate your goals and their operation on a scale of 1 to 10 for each of the guidelines.

B. If you do not have a set of goals, formulate a complete set using the Seven Guidelines as a guide.

1. Identify your purpose in life.
2. Choose goals that are consistent with the way you see yourself.
3. Write down your goals and set definite timetables for reaching them.
4. Break your goals down into easily achievable objectives.
5. Make your dreams come true. Make your goals happen.
6. Review your goals and check your progress.
7. Constantly set new goals.

"Thank the Lord!" he sighed as he settled back to relax.

But as he sat there, a question began to nibble at him: "What do I do now?"

Eventually, the letter carrier came whistling down the road, threw up his hand, waved, and walked on by. There were no letters for the man.

"Please tell me," the man asked, "What place is this?"

"Why, don't you know?" replied the letter carrier cheerfully, "This is Hell!"

One thing you will find for sure: At the top of every ladder of success, there is the bottom of another ladder. I hope you set a goal to always set a new goal with each success.

KEEP YOUR GOALS IN SIGHT

Florence Chadwick decided that she would become the first woman ever to swim the English Channel. For years she trained and desciplined herself to keep going long after her body cried out for relief. Finally, in 1952, the big day came. She set out full of hope, surrounded by newspeople and well-wishers in small boats. And, of course, there were the skeptics who doubted she'd make it.

As she neared the coast of England, a heavy fog settled in, and the waters became increasingly cold and choppy.

"Come on, Florence," encouraged her mother as she handed food to her, "You can make it! It's only a few more miles!"

Finally, exhausted, she asked to be pulled aboard the boat—just a few hundred yards from her goal. She was defeated and heart-broken; especially when she discovered how close she had been to reaching her goal.

"I'm not offering excuses," she later told news reporters, "But I think I could have made it, if I had been able to see my goal."

But Florence Chadwick was not so easily beaten. She decided to try again. This time, she concentrated on developing a mental image of the coast of England. She memorized every feature of the distant coast and fixed it clearly in her mind. On the appointed day, she encountered all of the choppy waters and fog that she had met before, but she made it. She became the first woman in history to swim the English Channel. Why? Because she could clearly see her goal—through her mind's eye!

Everything we do takes time. But, if we know where we are going, and we are steadily making progress toward our goals, we can accomplish amazing things with our lives.

Be patient but persistent in pursuing your goals!

But What If You Don't Make Your Goals?

Many of the greatest contributions were made by people who set out to do something entirely different. Technically, you'd have to say they didn't make their goals, but our world is a better place to live in because they made certain discoveries and contributions while pursuing their goals. Christopher Columbus, for example, set out to discover a new trade route to India. He missed by half a globe! Yet few of us who enjoy living in America would call him a failure.

All you really need to know is that you gave life your best shot. The value of pursuing goals is in the trying, in the doing, in the reaching out to achieve and to create. If you commit yourself to worthwhile goals, and vigorously pursue them, success will take care of itself.

chapter nine
TIME: YOUR GREATEST TREASURE

The most common complaint of some of the top salespeople and business leaders in this country is, "I simply don't have enough time!" A popular sign around offices these days reads, "The Hurrier I Go, The Behinder I Get." Do you ever feel that way?

Apparently, many people do! They go as hard as they can go, from early morning until they drop into bed at night. Yet they never seem to have enough time to get done everything they want to do, or feel they need to do.

If you feel like that, I have good news and bad news! The bad news is that you are not going to get any more time. There will always be only 24 hours in a day and only seven days in a week. But the good news is this: *You don't really need more time!*

TIME MARCHES ON!

Time is like money in the bank in many ways. There is, however, one significant difference between time and money. You can collect money and put it into a savings account—even let it draw interest for you. If you don't choose to invest it, you can simply leave it alone. Time is different. Your life is given to you one second at a time. Sure, you can do things to shorten or to lengthen the amount of time in your life.

But you simply can't stop time! You might take the watch from your arm and dash it on the pavement—but time marches on!

You might carry out your fantasy of smashing the alarm clock with a hammer—but time marches on! Jerk the calendar from the wall and throw it into the trash—but the days keep rolling by! For you, time will stop only when you die! There are no pauses in time!

YOU CAN CONTROL ONLY ONE THING!

If you cannot control time, there's only one thing you can control in relation to time—*the way you spend your time!* Time is yours to invest any way you choose. You can invest it in the pursuit of your goals and objectives; you can give it away in the pursuit of someone else's goals, or you can simply throw it away. The choice is always yours.

Taking charge of your life means that you choose how you will invest every second you are given. It does no good to fix the blame for never having enough time. It is useless to blame your job, the demands of other people, the circumstances of your life, or any other thief that steals those precious minutes out of your life. The only solution lies in fixing the problem. And there's only one way to do that—*Take complete charge of the time you are given!*

Peter Drucker has been called the "Father of American Management" because he has contributed so much to our understanding of how to run businesses and organizations. He says, "Time is the scarcest resource and unless it is managed nothing else can be managed." If that is true of businesses, it is equally true of our personal lives.

To manage your time you must master your habits. We are all creatures of habit. If you don't believe it, take this little test:

1. When you brush your teeth, which do you pick up first—the toothpaste or the toothbrush?
2. When you get into your automobile, do you place your foot on the brake or the accelerator first?
3. Which shoe do you always put on first?
4. Which side of your hair do you comb or brush first?
5. Which arm do you put into a coat first?

Our brains are programmed like giant computers to enable us to do routine things without thinking about them. If we don't consciously program routine activities, they program themselves. The only choice we have with habits is that we can decide which habits we program into our minds. And nowhere is this more crucial than in the area of managing our time.

PLANNING—THE MASTER KEY
TO EFFECTIVE TIME MANAGEMENT

The best way to control your habits, and therefore your life, is through a *systematic strategy of applied consistency*. In simpler terms, plan your life, and live your plan.

"But, I don't want to live a regimented life!" protested a woman in one of my seminars on time management. "I don't want to feel like every minute of my life has to be lived on a rigid schedule."

"Do you watch television sometimes?" I asked.

"Yes," she replied, "Almost every night."

"Do you ever watch programs you did not intend to watch when you sat down?" I queried.

"Well, yes," came the answer.

"Then, I continued, "Aren't you allowing television to impose a regimen on your life?"

"I guess so," she responded. "I never really thought about it."

"You can be sure that the network programmers have a very sophisticated strategy to get you to watch television with an applied consistency," I pointed out. "Whether you respond to their regimentation or to your own, you are following someone's schedule."

Let me ask you an important question: Are you a "flounder person" or a "trout person"? To help you formulate your answer, let's take a look at the characteristics of each fish.

The Flounder:
Lies on the bottom of the sea waiting for its food to come along
    Allows the tides to control its movements
        Does not resist natural forces
            Can be easily caught

The Trout:
Swims against the currents
  Chooses carefully what it will eat
    Decides when to resist and when to rest
      Is very hard to catch

Correspondingly:

- The "flounder person" reacts only to what comes his or her way, whereas the "trout person" acts with forethought and self-discipline.
- The "flounder person" waits for something to happen, while the "trout person" makes things happen.
- The "flounder person" concentrates on activities, and the "trout person" concentrates on goals and objectives.

POINTERS FOR
EFFECTIVE TIME MANAGEMENT

If you have decided that you want to take charge of your life by controlling your habits—rather than allowing them to control you—here are some pointers that can be helpful.

POINTER 1
Clarify Your Objectives

Goals are not the same as objectives. A *goal* is like a target you wish to hit, the end you'd like to reach. An *objective* is a step you take toward reaching your goal. For example, if your goal is to become more effective in managing your time, your most immediate objective is to read this chapter.

So, clarifying your objectives means deciding what steps you need to take to reach your goals, estimating how much time each step will take, and allotting the required time to complete the step. To do this, you need *a carefully designed activity schedule*.

Benefits of an Activity Schedule. By scheduling your activities carefully, you can control the way you spend your time—whether it's for fun or profit:

1. You can allot time according to your priorities.
2. You can spend your time on things you feel are worthwhile.
3. You can have more time to relax.
4. You can meet important deadlines.
5. You can constantly move toward your goals.
6. You can avoid wasted efforts.
7. You can be more flexible.
8. You can eliminate tasks that others should do.
9. You can have the peace of mind from knowing the really important things will get done.
10. You can enjoy leisure time activities, knowing that you have allocated all the time needed to do what is required.
11. You can work more comfortably and effectively on one thing at a time, knowing that everything will get done in the order of its priority.
12. You can work at your most comfortable and productive pace.

Adopt a Time Budget. Putting yourself on a time budget is one of the most liberating experiences you'll ever have. When you budget your available money, you make certain choices based on your fixed expenses each month, which you have to maintain. If you find these fixed expenses are out of proportion to your available income, you look for ways to reduce them. Usually, some money is left over for you to spend as you wish. The wise person invests some of it on the future and then enjoys buying the things that make life pleasant.

With a controlled time budget, you can accomplish the things you feel you should and still have time to spend as you wish. In other words, you can take breaks as you feel you need them, not when you get the chance. And you can relax better during the time you have allocated for relaxation.

Of course, you need to build flexibility into your time budget. One way to do so is to decide, in advance, where lost time will be made up later in your schedule. For example, if you have allocated one hour to a task and it takes an hour and fifteen minutes, you can take five minutes off of a scheduled break, and five minutes off each of the next two projects. By deciding in advance how to make up lost time, you find yourself more readily resisting the urge to goof off. You also find yourself evaluating how interruptions interfere with reaching your goals and looking for ways to minimize them.

At first, the idea of living by an activity plan and time budget seems a little mechanical, but, as you work at it, it becomes more natural. You'll love it because you will find that you are getting more done in less time, and you are more able to relax during your free time.

POINTER 2
Analyze Your Time Habits

How do you spend your time? Time robbers lurk around every corner of our lives, waiting to snatch away our precious minutes. To become effective persons and have enough time to relax, we must catch those thieves and put a stop to their tricks.

Keep a Time Log. One way to analyze your time habits is to keep a time log for the next two or three weeks. Write down how much time you spend doing each task, taking each break, and dealing with each interruption.

You might make some interesting discoveries. For example, you might discover that you waste time the same way during a specified time frame every day. You can plug up that hole and have more time to pursue your goals and to relax.

Another interesting discovery many people make is that they are more productive at various times of the day. Thus, they are able to schedule activities that require greater productivity during those peak times. If you find that you are more creative during certain hours, you can allocate the activities that require your greatest creativity during those hours, thereby saving the more mundane tasks for times when you are less creative.

Watch your activities—not the clock! Set daily and hourly goals in terms of results—not in terms of activities! Identify those nasty little habits of time-wasting and eliminate them. Here is a list of the more common time thieves:

1. Procrastination—putting things off until they end up requiring more time or until they gang up and take control of your schedule.
2. Trying to complete tasks for which you don't have enough information.

3. Doing unnecessary routine work—just because you have always done it.
4. Unnecessary distractions or interruptions.
5. Sloppy use of the telephone.
6. Unnecessary meetings, or meetings that last too long.
7. Failure to delegate tasks to capable people.
8. Lack of self-discipline in matters of time.
9. Failure to set priorities.
10. Unnecessary shuffling of mail and paperwork.
11. Excessive socializing.
12. Lack of mental control or concentration—daydreaming at the wrong times.
13. Lack of knowledge about your job.
14. Stretching our refreshment breaks.
15. Refusing to say"no" to things that interfere with your priorities.
16. Making careless mistakes that necessitate redoing work.
17. Sloppy or ineffective communications.
18. Failure to use management aids (like dictating machines, message centers, and the like) to full advantage.
19. Bulky, poorly designed systems or procedures.
20. Failure to insist that your co-workers carry their part of the load.

As you analyze your own time habits, you might find that many of the most common time thieves steal valuable time from you. You might also discover others that are not on the list. In any case, identify them as the enemy and declare war on them. After all, *it is your life they are stealing*!

POINTER 3
Keep a Daily and Weekly "To Do" List

At the end of every day, Charles Schwab, the famous past-president of Bethlehem Steel Company, made it a practice to invest five minutes analyzing the various problems he should tackle the next day. He would write down those tasks in the order of their priority. When he arrived at the office the next morning, he would start with task number 1 as soon as he got in. When he had completed that task, he would move on to tasks 2, 3, 4, and 5 in order.

"This is the most practical lesson I've ever learned," said the multimillionaire. He gave this example to prove his point: "I had put off a phone call for nine months so I decided to list it as my number one task on my next day's agenda. That call netted us $2 million because of a new order for steel beams." From that moment, he was totally committed to the concept.

Benefits of a "To Do" List
1. It frees your mind from the nagging worry that there is something important you are overlooking.
2. It aids relaxation by giving you a definite time to do what is important.
3. It assumes that crucial deadlines are met.
4. It keeps you from wasting time on marginal activities.
5. It releases you to do your best on the task at hand.
6. It helps you to keep from becoming a workaholic.
7. It helps you to communicate effectively with other people what you consider most important.
8. It gives you a logical place to start and stop each day.
9. It helps you to assure other people that their concerns will be dealt with.
10. It aids in establishing a systematic flow of productivity and helps you work at a controlled pace.
11. It helps you to resist unnecessary interruptions.
12. It helps you to avoid procrastination.

In short, by formulating a daily and weekly "to do" list, you choose how to spend your days, rather than waiting to react to what happens. And it helps you avoid the stress and frustration of working yourself to death and getting little accomplished.

One of the greatest satisfactions I get out of life is the feeling of accomplishment that comes each time I check off another task on my "to do" list. I can look at that list at the end of the day and readily determine whether or not I have been an effective person. Since I don't like to feel like an ineffective person, I live by that "to do" list. Try it! You'll like it!

POINTER 4
Get Yourself Organized

Some of the most disorganized people in the world are among the hardest workers. They work like crazy all day, conscientiously try to get everything done, and leave their offices tense because of important letters unwritten, people unseen, and urgent projects unfinished.

One reason they work longer and harder than everyone else is that they reinvent the wheel every time they need a ride. They have to put forth extra effort because they do everything in a haphazard way. Often they justify their disorganization on the grounds that they like their freedom to do things the way they want to do them.

Organization can be a great aid to personal freedom, if you make it work for you rather than vice versa. It can help you work more easily, get more done in less time, and make you more valuable to any organization.

Cultivate Decisiveness. One reason that people stay disorganized is that they hate to make decisions. For this reason they are often overlooked when promotion time comes around.

Once, before mechanical sorters were invented, the manager of an apple orchard needed a sorter to separate the apples into three sizes. Logically, he selected the best picker he had and promoted him to the position. Before the picker were placed three baskets, each for a different size. The pickers would bring their apples and pile them on a large table beside him, and he was to sort them into the baskets.

Knowing the fellow to be a good worker, the manager left him at work and went to town. Upon his return, he was shocked to see a mountain of apples completely covering the table and falling off on all sides. There, before the empty baskets, sat his new sorter—with an apple in each hand and a puzzled look on his face. He was a great picker, but he simply couldn't make a decision as to whether an apple was big, little, or middle-sized. Of course, he lost his promotion.

If you expect to advance in your career, you stand a much better chance of moving up if you learn how to handle responsibility. In other words, the better you can make decisions, the more promotable you become. Cultivate the ability to decide on priorities, on how the various pieces of work fit together, and on how to orchestrate your efforts and the efforts of others.

Process Papers— Don't Shuffle Them. How many times do you

look at a piece of paper, or a letter, before you decide what to do with it and then do it? I have been amazed at how much time I can save, and how much more smoothly my work flows, since I started handling papers only once.

Here's how it works for me. I set aside a time for reading and answering mail. I read each letter, decide what action it calls for, and immediately dictate an answer. I simply refuse to keep a "later file" on my desk. As a result, I get more done in less time, worry less about what I'm going to do, and keep other people happier. It really works!

Keep Your Desk, and Your Life, Uncluttered. Did you ever stop to think that your desk would probably tell a character analyst more about you than your handwriting, your photograph, or the lines in your palm? Efficiency experts have learned from studies that people who have cluttered desks tend to have cluttered lives. In every area of life, they leave jobs half-done or not started at all. As a result, they get less done and spend more time doing everything they do.

We spend most of our lives at work. Yet our work can become drudgery if we allow it to bog down. You can make your work an adventure by reducing your tasks to their simplest form and doing them in the order of their priority. In seminars, I often recommend the KISMIF system of getting yourself organized. KISMIF stands for "Keep It Simple, Make It Fun." The way to execute this system is to start it first thing in the morning and follow it through all day. For example, set the alarm for precisely the time you need to get out of bed and get up at that time. Many people make the decision to get up at least ten times each morning. They could rid themselves of nine decisions every day by doing what they have decided to do.

If an activity is important in relation to your goals, do it! If it's not, forget it and move on! Clean your desk and your life of all the clutter it has collected—not by putting it all in the trash can but by getting today's work done today.

POINTER 5
Cultivate the Time Management Habit

What would you do if someone gave you a million dollars? The first thing you'd probably do is protect it. You certainly wouldn't leave it in clear view on the front seat of your car. And you wouldn't break it up into small bills and hand it out to everybody you meet. Isn't it ironic that some people protect their money and possessions with their lives, yet let their lives slip away with little thought? They don't seem to realize that *time* is their most valuable possession. No one has more time than you do. Each of us is given 1,440 minutes each day, 168 hours each week, and 8,760 hours every year. Here are some tips to help you protect the valuable gift of time that you are given each day:

Use Every Minute to Pursue Your Goals. For example, what do you do when you are caught in a traffic jam? Noel Coward didn't fuss and fume; he took out a piece of paper and wrote his popular song, "I'll See You Again." Many successful people keep self-help cassettes handy to listen to while they are driving, selected reading materials available to use while waiting for someone, and routine paperwork handy—just to salvage time lost to delays.

Do Everything Right the First Time. "Why is there never enough time to do something right, but always enough time to do it over?" is a familiar question.

Manage Visitors—Don't Let Them Manage You. If you have a secretary, authorize him or her to screen your visitors and set up appointments for you. Meet visitors outside your door so you can leave if you feel they are wasting your time. Confer standing up, and limit the length of the interview. Organize the interview so that you get business handled quickly; then terminate the visit.

Keep Time in Meetings to a Minimum. Attend only meetings that are necessary. Insist on starting on time, getting and sticking to the point, limiting the agenda, and ending on time. Meetings are great time wasters.

Learn to Delegate Responsibility and Authority to competent people working with you.

Control Your Telephone Usage. If possible, block your phone calls together. Set aside time to talk on the phone, and limit your call to the allotted time.

POINTER 6
Take Time for All Your
Goals—Including Leisure

You are *a total person*. You need time to recharge your batteries through rest and recreation, time to cultivate relationships that matter, time to learn and grow, and time to enjoy the beauty of God's great world. If you're like most of us, unless you allocate an appropriate amount of time, you'll find that the things that make life worth living get relegated to second place—and usually lose out to life's urgencies. I like this anonymous piece of prose:

- Allow time for work; it's the price of success.
- Allow time for love; it's the sacrament of life.
- Allow time to play; it's the secret of youth.
- Allow time to read; it's the foundation of knowledge.

Exercise 9–1. "Saving" Time

Annual Income	Each Hour Is Worth	Each Minute Is Worth	In a Year An Hour Per Day Saved Is Worth
$10,000	$5.16	$.0864	$1259
12,000	6.16	.1024	1503
14,000	7.16	.1192	1748
16,000	8.16	.1360	1992
20,000	10.32	.1728	2518
25,000	12.81	.2134	3125
30,000	15.37	.2561	3750
35,000	17.93	.2988	4375
40,000	20.64	.3596	5036
50,000	25.62	.4268	6250
75,000	38.42	.6403	9374
100,000	51.24	.8536	12,500
125,000	64.03	1.067	15,623
150,000	76.84	1.280	18,749
175,000	89.65	1.494	21,875
200,000	102.45	1.707	24,998

Note: The table is based on 244 work days of 8 hours each.

By saving one hour each working day during a normal career, you can add the equivalent of six years of productivity. That's better than early retirement at full benefits!

- Allow time to help and enjoy friends; it's the source of happiness.
- Allow time to dream; it keeps your hopes alive.
- Allow time to laugh; it's the spice of life.
- Allow time to worship; it's the highway of reverence.
- Allow time to pray; it helps bring God near and washes the dust of the earth from your eyes.

Taking charge of your life means that you assume responsibility for managing your time. It means that you make time work for you, rather than becoming a slave to the clock. Learn to manage your time and you can reach your goals—and enjoy your life.

Using the chart in Exercise 9–1, determine how much money you could save by saving one hour each working day for the next year. Think of something you could buy with the money you waste on lost time.

chapter ten
HOW TO MOVE THE BIGGEST OBSTACLE: YOURSELF

Daniel Webster told a story from his childhood that describes how unmotivated some people are. Daniel and his brother, Ezekiel, were sitting in the shade one day when their father approached.

"Watcha' doin', Ezekiel?" asked the father.

"Nuthin!" replied Ezekiel.

"Well, what are you doing, Daniel?"

"Helpin' Zeke!" came the casual response.

Obviously, Daniel Webster didn't spend the remainder of his life "helpin' " somebody do "nuthin'." He spent more than fifty years in great demand as an orator, lawyer, and statesman.

People are known for what they finish, not for what they start.

THE BEST LAID SCHEMES O' MICE AN' MEN . . .

Nothing we have said so far in this book works unless you do! The "best laid schemes," the most elaborate plans, and the highest of intentions are of no value until someone makes them become reality. You can read motivational books and listen to motivational speeches and cassettes until high-sounding phrases roll off your tongue like water from Niagara. But nothing worthwhile happens until you do something with what you have read and heard.

The crying need today is not for more knowledge. The so-called "knowledge explosion" is mushrooming so fast that if you could read a book each day for the remainder of your life, you'd be more than a million years behind in your reading when you died.

What the world needs is action—constructive action by intelligent people of good will!

GEARED FOR POWER . . .

"How much horsepower does that thing have?" I asked the man who had just shut down a bulldozer, which had been chewing up an old house as if it were made of straw.

"It's got sixty horsepower," he replied nonchalantly.

"Only sixty?" I exclaimed.

"Surprised, huh?" he chuckled with that look that told me he'd seen the same response before. "I'll bet you're thinking your Mercedes has more than twice that many horses," he mused.

"You're right," I said.

"Not only that," he continued, "your car will run at least forty times as fast and get about ten times as many miles per gallon of fuel."

"But my car won't chew up buildings," I responded.

"It's all in the transmission," he explained. "This baby's geared for power. You see, it's not how much power you've got that counts, but how you use it!"

Leaving, I thanked him for his valuable lesson, with that sentence running over and over in my mind: *"It's not how much power you've got that counts, but how you use it!"* When we consider the power in our minds, in our personalities, in our talents and abilities, each of us has more power than we could ever use. As I started the motor in my car, I listened to the quiet purr of all that power. Then it occurred to me that the car would sit there all day and eventually run out of gas, unless I put the transmission into gear. I slipped it into gear, gently pressed on the accelerator, and moved on toward my destination.

That's the key, isn't it? *Power is useless until it is applied.* Once you act, the power inside you will take you toward your destination. Action unlocks the door to success in any venture.

THE ENEMY IS US

Occasionally, that great philosopher of the comic strip, Pogo, has a way of putting his finger (or "claw" if you prefer) right on the problem. Once, after trying to fight a battle that did not exist, he gave us this bit of insight: "We have met the enemy, and the enemy is us!" Thoreau said it a little more poetically: "As long as a man stands in his own way, everything seems to be in his way." In other words, the greatest obstacle in our way on the road to success is ourselves. How to apply the power that lies within us to move that obstacle is a question of considerable importance.

"Nido," said a young saleswoman who was about to be discharged due to her repeated failures to meet quotas, "I know everything I need to know to become a good salesperson. I know my company and its products. I know how to sell. I know my territory. I come to these meetings and get all charged up. Then I get back into the field and I just can't get going."

I assured that young woman that she was not the only person who had ever felt that way. Here are some tips I gave her to help her get her life on track toward her goals. Perhaps you will find them useful.

TIP 1
Motivation Without Mobilization Means Frustration

"Don't just stand there! Do something!"

To this often heard exclamation, the logical response is, "What should I do?"

Unfortunately (or perhaps fortunately), nobody can tell you what you should do. Only you know what your goals are. Many of the people I encounter are frustrated because they want to be great salespeople, great secretaries, or great managers, but they don't know how to move their greatest obstacles —themselves. They are *motivated, but not mobilized*.

To mobilize, according to Mr. Webster, means "to put into action or motion." The word, adapted from military terminology, once carried the idea of "marshalling troops for a specific battle." Carefully disciplined soldiers going into combat have two main objectives: first to defeat the enemy, and second to stay alive. Those priorities might sound exactly the opposite of those that most of us would set if we were going into combat. However, those who put their cause and their country first are often called "heroes" or "patriots." Those who think primarily about their own safety are called "cowards" or "deserters."

I'm not trying to make a soldier out of you, but merely point out a very important principle that can change your outlook on life: *What you do is often more important than how much you do!* Those who adopt the song "Stayin' Alive" as their credo for life, might do just that, but whether they will ever do much more than that is doubtful. If your preocupation in life is to remain comfortable, to do what you're told, to do what feels good, or to keep doing only what you are expected to do, you will probably be just as frustrated ten years from now as you are right now.

Virtually every great achievement of history was preceded by an intense effort by the achiever to accomplish a goal—regardless of the personal cost, the loss of comfort, or the opinions of others. These achievers marshalled their inner resources in a specific direction to accomplish definite objectives. They put their personal power in gear and steered it in the direction of their goal.

Mobilizing yourself involves three basic steps:

1. Decide what you want most to achieve.
2. Determine the first step toward getting what you want.
3. Do the first thing that will move you toward what you want.

Let's look at these steps a little more in detail.

Step 1:
Decide What You Want Most to Achieve

We devoted a whole chapter to the value of setting goals and to making goals work for you. You may have even done the exercise at the end of the chapter. If not, I urge you to go back and do it. If, however, your goals are already written out, broken down into manageable objectives, and reduced to specific tasks with definite deadlines, and if you still can't get yourself moving toward them, your goals probably do not adequately reflect what you really want most to do with your life.

A middle-aged minister once barricaded himself inside his

home and threatened to shoot anyone who tried to get to him. The incident mystified members of his congregation because they described him as a "loving and faithful minister" whose only problem had been that he had had difficulty staying very long in his last three parishes. As the story unravelled, it became apparent that the man had chosen the ministry only because the ministry was a family tradition—not because he really wanted to do it. What he really wanted, he later said, was to teach mathematics in a high school.

What a sad yet all-too-familiar story! Far too many people get locked into doing things that they really don't want to do; then they try to "make the best of a bad situation."

Probably the most decisive factor in determining whether or not you will reach your goals is the intensity of your desire to reach those goals. *It's important to be doing what is important to you.*

Mobilizing yourself involves focusing, and keeping clearly in focus, precisely what you want to achieve. Goals have value only when they are very personal to you.

Step 2:
Determine the First Step Toward What You Want

If taking the first step of a journey is important, then taking that step in the right direction is equally important. Imagine how much of a problem NASA would have had recruiting astronauts for their first moon shot if they had not had a clear plan drawn up. "We have decided we want to go to the moon," they might have said. "But we're not sure exactly how to get there. We're going to try out a few things to see if they will work. We might lose a few people along the way, but that's the price you pay for progress." Any person foolish enough to enlist in such a venture would probably have been disqualified due to a lack of intelligence. Instead, NASA used the opposite approach. The administrators broke their goals down into manageable objectives and planned carefully the first step that had to be taken.

One of the greatest reasons people cannot mobilize themselves is that they try to do great things. Most worthwhile achievements are a result of many little things done in a single direction.

Dreaming of owning a large and beautiful house someday is one thing. Quite another thing is digging the foundation for that house, making the sale that will move you closer to a down payment, or putting $100 into your savings account to be used for only that purpose. As long as our goals are so distant that they are only idle dreams, we are not likely to gear up the power within us to reach out for them.

Mobilizing yourself involves deciding what you want, then determining what will get you what you want. That leads us to the third step.

Step 3: Do the First Thing That Will Move You Toward Your Goal

Do what will get you what you want. Do *only* what will get you what you want. "Our main business is not to see what lies dimly at a distance;" said Thomas Carlyle, "but to do what lies clearly at hand." Many people have trouble getting themselves off dead center because none of the things they must do will move them closer toward their goals. They may try to kick themselves into doing something, but they will never be successful because kicking themselves becomes increasingly painful.

Even the most routine chores become palatable when we know they are leading us toward the realization of our goals. If you have to kick yourself to get out of bed every morning, check to see if what you are doing all day is in the direction of your goals. For example, William James, a noted psychologist, often observed that, "The minute anything becomes personal with anyone, it becomes the most interesting thing in the world." To illustrate his point, he would ask his students to consider a timetable. What could be duller than a timetable? Yet, he would point out, when you are planning a trip, it is hard to find anything more interesting. The change comes about when the timetable enters your life in a personal way.

But remember, nothing works unless you do! Do what will get you what you want. Breaking out of a pattern of doing what somebody else expects you to do might be uncomfortable at first. Often you have to take the first step before the second step becomes clear to you. Uncertainty and risk are great deterrents to action. Just trust your goals, and your ability to achieve them, enough to take the first step. As you do, the second step will become clearer to you. One thing seems fairly certain; if you shoot at nothing, you'll hit it every time.

To mobilize yourself, decide what you want, determine what will get you what you want, then act—do what will get you what you want most to achieve. Motivation without mobilization means only frustration.

TIP 2
Keep Your Perspective in Perspective

The way you view what lies ahead of you often makes the difference in whether you will get yourself moving in the right direction or continue to do nothing toward reaching your goals. For example, "The only person who behaves sensibly," said George Bernard Shaw, "is my tailor. He takes new measurements every time he sees me. All the rest go on with their old measurements." David might have said, "Goliath is just too big for me to fight with this little slingshot." But he apparently decided that the giant was too big for him to miss. Recently, I saw a sign in a bustling business establishment that said, "We hear there is a recession—we have decided not to participate." I like that!

"Perspective" is defined as "a point of view." The word also means "a view of things in their true relationship or relative importance." Here are some pointers to help you keep your perspective in perspective.

Pointer 1: Learn to Take the Long View

Cultivate the art of looking at events in their proper relationship to your whole life. Often something appears for the moment to be a tragedy, but it becomes only a minor annoyance when taken in the context of your total life.

Sometimes even problems that cause major difficulty turn out to be very positive developments. For example, while in Enterprise, Alabama, for a speaking engagement, I was taken to see the town's trademark—a large statue of a boll weevil.

"Why a boll weevil?" I asked.

"Many years ago," replied my host, "the entire economy of Enterprise was based on raising cotton. It was a poor little farming community with no future. Then, for several years in a row, the boll weevil wiped out the entire cotton crop for miles around. The people were starving."

"Someone stepped forward," he continued, "and suggested the town diversify its crops and try to attract some industries. That's exactly what happened, and you see the result—a thriving, broad-based economy. Had it not been for the boll weevil, we'd still be tied to cotton. He's our hero!"

If you could view your life as you do a highway from an airliner, many of the detours and curves would make more sense. The value of taking the long view of life is that it enables you to see problems as opportunities, passing up the fun-for-the-moment to pursue a worthwhile goal.

Pointer 2: Learn to Take the Positive View

"Two people looked out from prison bars: one person saw only mud, the other person saw the stars."

There are two kinds of people in the world: the optimists and the pessimists. Hold up a glass of water, and the pessimist says, "It's half empty," while the optimist says, "It's half full." Pessimists say, "I can't," so they don't try. Optimists say, "I can" and at least try. Someone has said that "I can't" actually means "I won't try!"

Taking the positive view requires more than simply casting out negative thoughts—although that is an important part of it. Positive input must replace negative thoughts. In fact, the quickest way to cast out negative thoughts is to feed enough positive thoughts into your mind that there is no longer room for the negative thoughts. People who take the positive view basically see the world as a good place. They actively look for the good in other people and in situations, and they act with hope and faith.

Pointer 3: Focus on Your Winnings

Most of us tend to react more sharply to pain than we do to pleasure. We therefore tend to feel more intensely our losses, failures, our difficulties than we do our wins, our gains, our joys. You are probably better at what you do than you realize, if you could remember how well you have been doing it.

Here's a way to keep your perspective: Keep score on your victories. Write down your "winnings" on a list, and keep the list where you can review it often. Collect momentos of your victories, including pictures, newspaper clippings, awards, and the like. You might be surprised at how many of these things you can legitamately gather.

Remember, it is always easier to "curse the darkness" than it is to "light a candle."

Pointer 4: Learn to Be Flexible

A giant skyscraper might sway as much as six or eight feet in either direction. If it didn't have that much flexibility, it would break under the force of a strong wind. Likewise, people who become "married" to a single viewpoint tend to become increasingly frightened by anything that seems to threaten that position. Your creativity in solving problems, and in taking advantage of opportunities, is often related directly to the amount of flexibility you have.

For example, many farmers sat around and complained about the increasing cost of electricity, and the unpleasantness of disposing of all the fertilizer that their cows generated. But the Waybright brothers, who with their brother-in-law run the Mason Dixon Farms near Gettysburg, Pennsylvania, decided to quit complaining and start generating—electricity, that is. They have constructed a power generator that uses methane gas produced by heated cow manure from their herd of 2,000. With this generator, they have succeeded in cutting their annual power bill from $30,000 to $15,000.

Inflexibility caused the surrounding farmers to laughingly call the project "Waybright's folly." But no one is laughing any longer. In fact, agriculture ministers from around the world, congressmen, and farmers are streaming to the Waybright farm to see how it's done. Soon the Waybright Brothers expect to sell some excess power to their neighbors. And that's no bull!

TIP 3
Master Your Emotions; Don't Let Them Master You

The drug addict, the alcoholic, and the habitual criminal all have one thing in common: They have allowed their feelings to dominate them.

"I don't feel any different than I did when I came in here," a young woman said to me at the close of one of my motivational seminars. "I guess I'm not cut out to be a highly motivated person. I've read so many books, and heard so many tapes, that I know all the reasons for becoming a real go-getter . . . but I just don't feel like doing anything!"

As she reeled off the list of books she'd read, it became obvious that she'd missed most of what the writers had said.

"What have you done about what you have read?" I asked.

"I've tried to change my attitude," she protested, "but I've got to be honest with myself—I just don't feel any different!"

"The way you feel has little to do with your success or failure," I told her.

"What do you mean?" she asked.

"If I handed you an envelope and told you it contained a million dollars, would you hand it back to me and tell me it didn't feel like it had a million dollars in it?" I asked.

"No!" was her quick response, "I'd open it to see if you were telling me the truth!"

After a long pause, a smile broke on her face.

"Now I get it!" she said with a look of triumph, "I wouldn't know if it were true until I checked it out—no matter how I felt!"

Our emotions are our least dependable, and often our most deceptive, sensing devices. What the wise old masters have told us in a thousand ways boils down to this: *It is easier to act your way into feeling the way you want to feel than it is to feel your way into acting the way you want to act!* In other words, *master your feelings; don't let them master you*:

- If you work only on days you feel like working, you'll never amount to much.
- If you do your best only when you feel like doing your best, your work will probably be pretty shabby.

105

• If you take charge of your emotions, they will work for you, not against you.

Watch That Trap

Mark Twain once gave very sound advice to a group of young people who were working toward ambitious goals. "Keep away from people who try to belittle your ambitions," he said. "Small people always do that, but the really great make you feel that you, too, can become great." If you would be successful, walk and talk with successful people.

TIP 4
Make Time Work for, Not Against You

How you use your time today is important, because you are exchanging a day of your life for it. "Remember," said Thomas a Kempis, "that lost time does not return."

Killing time is hard work. Time might fly when you're having fun—that is, when you are busily engaged in pursuing worthwhile goals—but it can drag when you are just killing time—doing busy work or simply putting in hours. Yet it is amazing to me how hard some people work at killing time.

Start Early Each Day. "The early morning hath gold in its mouth," said Benjamin Franklin.

Have you ever noticed that the first few waking moments of a day tend to set a pattern for the remainder of that day? "I overslept this morning," said a comedian, "and in the rush to get started, I burned my toast, spilled coffee all over my suit, and cut myself shaving. My neighbor's dog bit me while I was rushing to my car—which wouldn't start. . . . From there, the day seemed to go downhill!"

To some people, every morning is "the morning after."

But what a difference when we awaken early, refreshed after a good night's sleep, with something exciting to do first thing! It gives us time to greet God, to welcome the new day with all its exciting possibilities, and to get in touch with the inner resources that enable us to take on the challenging prospects lying before us. I like to greet the day with the feeling expressed in the old saying,

"This is the first day of the rest of my life." Yesterday, with all its frets and worries, ended when I fell asleep last night. Today is a new day, a fresh new page on which I can write some fine moments, if I only try.

The best time to move your greatest obstacle—yourself—is first thing in the morning.

Keep Moving. Make inertia work for you! "There is a condition or circumstance that has a greater bearing upon the happiness of life than any other," said John Burroughs. "It is to keep moving." He compares our lives to a stream of water. "If it stops, it stagnates," he concludes.

Remember, a body in motion tends to remain in motion, in the same direction, and at the same speed, unless acted upon by an outside force. For example, experts tell us that it takes less fuel to keep a car running, once it is in motion, than it does to get it started. Perhaps one reason some people are so tired at the end of a day is that they used up too much "fuel" trying to get themselves going after countless stops during the day.

Know What to Do Next. One secret of keeping your life moving is to always know what you are going to do next. As a case in point, a great writer once confessed that the most awesome thing for him was a blank piece of paper in the typewriter. So he developed a plan to counter the problem. Each day, when he was ready to quit writing, he would leave a piece of paper in the typewriter with a sentence half finished on it. The next morning, the first thing he would do was to finish that sentence. Soon he would be thoroughly engrossed in his writing and off to a productive day.

A "to do" list, an assignment neatly stacked on your desk, or a time schedule will serve the same purpose. Since confusion is one of the greatest hindrances to action, it helps to always know what you are going to tackle as soon as you finish every task.

TIP 4
Be a Self-Starter

Are you a thermometer or a thermostat? A thermometer only reflects the temperature of its environment, adjusting to the situation. But a thermostat initiates action to change the temperature in its environment. Correspondingly, losers only adjust to their situations. They do what seems to be expected of them. They react to their environments. But winners decide what needs to be done and take action. They drive their energies, and they are not driven by them. They learn how to push things through to a successful finish, then move on to the next task.

Avoid Excuses. Winners make their goals; losers make excuses. Take a look at some of the classic excuses people use to justify not being self-starters:

1. I didn't know what you wanted.
2. I didn't know you needed it right away.
3. I don't know how to do it.
4. I'm waiting for an okay.
5. That's not my job.
6. Wait until the boss gets back.
7. I forgot.
8. That's not the way we've always done it.
9. I just didn't get around to it.
10. I might do it wrong.

Successful, self-starting individuals seek responsibility. They take calculated risks. They don't make excuses to cover up their inactivity.

TIP 6
Give Everything You Do Everything You've Got

Dr. Peale is right! Enthusiasm does make the difference! In fact, Ralph Waldo Emerson said, "Nothing great was ever achieved without enthusiasm." And W. H. Sheldon said, "Happiness is essentially a state of going somewhere wholeheartedly."

What Is Enthusiasm? Enthusiasm is more than a "buzz word" for motivational speakers and writers. It is a way of life for those people who are achieving. "For as long as I can remember," confessed Samuel Goldwyn, the famous Hollywood producer, "whatever I was doing at the time was the most important thing in the world for me. . . . I have found enthusiasm for work to be the most priceless ingredient in any recipe for successful living."

Enthusiasm Is:
A positive inner force that makes things happen
A gracious and polite bid for attention
A method of diplomacy and persuasion
A cooperative spirit
An excitement for life

Enthusiasm comes from an ancient Greek word meaning "inspired." In modern dictionaries it is defined as: "A warmth of feeling: keen interest: fervor." To comprehend enthusiasm, imagine an artist doing a pencil sketch of a beautiful pastoral scene at sunset. When the sketch is completed, it is proportionally correct, exact in detail, and sharp in contrast. But it is dull and uninteresting because it lacks color, shading, warmth. Now the skilled artist takes brushes and plays light against shadows, adds colors and hues, and paints in depth and feeling. Suddenly the picture comes alive.

Enthusiasm is the color of inspiration and courage. It is the light of creativity and insight. It is the depth of emotion and the feeling of purpose.

Enthusiasm enables you to move your biggest obstacle— yourself!

How Do You Get Enthusiasm? Vince Lombardi is a name that is synonymous with enthusiasm in American life. When he took over the Green Bay Packers, they were on the bottom. In 1958, they lost 10 out of their 12 games, tied 1 and won 1. When they came to camp in June of 1959, the players were greeted by a new coach, Vince Lombardi.

"Gentlemen, we are going to have a football team," said the new coach, according to an article in *Guideposts Magazine*. "We are going to win some games. Get that!"

Now how were they going to do that?

"You are going to learn to block, run and tackle," he said. "You are going to outplay all the teams that come up against you."

Then he threw in the clincher!

"You are to have confidence in me and enthusiasm for my system," he ordered. "Hereafter, I want you to think of only three things: your home, your religion, and the Green Bay Packers! Let enthusiasm take ahold of you!"

What followed is great evidence that "enthusiasm is contagious." It did take ahold of them. With virtually the same players, they won seven games the next season. The following year, they won their division title, and the third year, they won the world championship. That team is often referred to as the "great dynasty" of professional football.

One Day at a Time. If you are having trouble getting yourself going, select the most important and "do-able" task available. Then let it become the focal point of your attention. Just for today, give it everything you've got! Then, again tomorrow, do the same thing. Eventually, it will become a beautiful and exciting pattern that will produce incredible results.

THE TIME IS NOW, THE PERSON IS YOU

If you've been sitting around waiting for a better opportunity, a better job, a better set of circumstances, recognize that waiting is a dead end street. For example, I'm sure you've seen the "distinguished world travelers" who approach people on the streets and ask for handouts. "There's a fellow coming in on the next train who owes me some money," they will tell you. "Can you loan me a dollar to get something to eat?" they ask. Two things are really sad about such scenes. First, many of them actually seem to believe what they are telling you, but somehow the person with the money never shows up. Second, their attitude is not that different from many people I meet at seminars and in firms where I'm called in as a consultant. You'll always find those people who are waiting for their opportunity to come along.

Losers wait for something to happen; winners make things happen! Winners decide that they will take charge of their lives, and not trust their futures to circumstances or situations in which they find themselves. If you want to move your greatest obstacle, realize that the obstacle is yourself—and that the time to act is now! Concentrate on developing the success habit, and create an atmosphere of success around yourself!

Remember, whatever keeps you from reaching your goal for today had better be important—it's costing you a day of your life!

Exercise 10 –1. Taking Steps

In this exercise, you have an opportunity to put into practice what we have talked about in this chapter.

1. Write down the first step you must take to begin moving toward your biggest goal:

   _____

   _____

   _____

2. List the three biggest reasons you have not taken this step before now:

   _____

   _____

   _____

3. Now write down a strategy for overcoming each of the three reasons:

   _____

   _____

   _____

4. Set a target date to complete the implementation of each of the three strategies:

   _____

   _____

   _____

chapter eleven
TO CATCH A THIEF

What would you do if you found yourself in the following situation?

When you return to your house tonight, you find that someone has been there in your absence—an intruder, a thief! Quickly, you search through your belongings and find only one thing of value missing. Although angry, you are relieved that nothing else was taken. Besides, you reason, the stolen item is covered by insurance.

But tomorrow night you discover that the thief has returned and taken only one thing of value. By now you are steaming mad, but you are still covered by insurance. Night after night you return home to find that, each day, the thief has returned and taken one thing you value. Soon your insurance is cancelled—so that each thing the thief takes costs you dearly. Moreover, you resent the theft of your hard-won possessions. Your neighbors say they never see the thief. And the police are mystified.

The question, What would you do?

You call a private investigation firm and ask if they can help.

"Certainly," says the chief detective, "I have six investigators I will put on it right away. Their names are Who, What, When, Where, Why, and How. They can catch any thief!"

Using these six investigators, let's see if we can capture the thief who steals something of far more value than items from your house—although this thief often steals money and things money can buy. Who is the thief? *Procrastination*! We will examine how procrastination robs us and what we can do to stop him.

WHO PROCRASTINATES?

First, *who procrastinates*? Unfortunately, almost all of us put off things we know we need to do, as well as things we want to do. Somehow we convince ourselves that we will have more time later or that the task will be easier at another time. But we never seem to have more time, and the task usually gets harder the longer we wait to tackle it.

For some people, procrastination becomes a way of life. As an illustration, a man found an old shoe ticket in a desk drawer he was cleaning out. Try as he may, he couldn't remember the pair of shoes it represented. So he concluded that it must be several years old. Out of curiosity, he stuck the shoe ticket into his pocket, and, on his way home that night, he stopped by the shoe shop. Without saying a word, he handed the ticket to the old cobbler. The old fellow studied the ticket for a minute, shuffled into the back room, and soon returned.

"They'll be ready next Wednesday!" he said with his usual unruffled smile.

An industry leader said to me recently that he wanted to promote a bright young salesperson who was working for him.

"But," he told me, "He never gets anything finished. His desk is full of unfinished reports, his log sheet is full of calls he *intended* to make, and he's always going to answer my memos *tomorrow*!

As I listened to this executive, I realized that there are many young women and men out there who could really go places if they would break the procrastination habit.

How big a problem is procrastination to you? Only you can answer this question because only you know how often you put things off. Furthermore, procrastination is a problem that only you can solve. *But you can solve it!*

Some of the leading figures in American life have made it big because they solved the problem of procrastination. Dr. Norman Vincent Peale, in *The Power of Positive Thinking*, describes how procrastination nearly swamped him until he did something about it. Here's his formula for arresting procrastination:

1. Pick one area where procrastination plagues you, and conquer it.
2. Learn to set priorities and focus on one problem at a time.

3. Give yourself deadlines.
4. Don't duck the most difficult problems.
5. Don't let perfectionism paralyze you. If you put everything off 'till you're sure of it, you'll never get anything done.

WHAT IS PROCRASTINATION?

Although procrastination is a thief of time, it is more than that. It is a nasty habit that robs us of our self-respect and the respect of others, that costs businesses many dollars, and that closes the door on opportunities.

Procrastination not only hinders our careers, it robs us in our personal lives. Often an encouraging word to a struggling friend somehow never gets said. An intended word of praise is never expressed. Or we never get around to that act of love we meant to do for someone. Procrastination steals such things from us and from those they could have helped.

What is procrastination? It is delaying anything you need or want to do, until later—when there is no valid reason to do so.

WHEN DO WE PROCRASTINATE?

For some of us, I fear the answer to that question is "far too often!" Snooze alarms, for example, start the day out on a note of procrastination for many people. They let you sleep for five minutes more, then five minutes more, then five minutes more. They must be popular because so many of them have been sold in recent years. Any day that starts with lying in bed—planning to get up later—is sure to be a day of putting things off. Once the pattern is set, it is hard to break.

Here are some tips that can help you get off to a good start each morning and keep fighting procrastination all day:

1. *Get ready for the next day before you retire*. Before you go to bed, lay out everything you need for the next morning. Set a fixed routine for getting started every morning so you won't have to make decisions first thing. Make sure you have something to look forward to, again first thing.

2. *Get a good night's sleep.* Allow enough time. Go to bed with nothing on your stomach and nothing on your mind. Too much food or drink in the evening will make you restless. Practice emptying your mind as you empty your pockets, so you can rest unworried.

3. *Use your alarm correctly.* Set it for the time you need to get up, and then get up when it goes off.

4. *Exercise first thing.* There's nothing like a vigorous workout to get your blood circulating and your body ready for the day.

5. *Greet the day in the way that appeals most to you.* Some people find awakening to be a shattering experience and need to start out slowly. Others find they can hit the ground running, and prefer to do it that way. Find the pattern that best suits you, and stick to it.

6. *Take some time early to get in touch with your inner resources.* Doing so helps to fill your mind with positive thoughts before it has time to follow the natural pattern of dreading the problems of the day.

7. *Have your whole day planned, and stick to your plan.* Having every minute planned, even though you may have to push aside your plans several times during that day, is better than always wondering what you will do next.

The only way to beat procrastination is to hit hard first thing in the morning, and stay after it all day, everyday!

WHERE DO WE PROCRASTINATE?

This question might sound odd because some people seem to procrastinate everywhere they go. But, unpleasantness seems to be linked very closely to putting things off. I talked with one person who had been a real go-getter while he was out in the field selling. He was so good that they promoted him to regional sales manager. As an executive, he found that he spent most of his time planning what he was going to do next.

As we talked, he discovered that he had enjoyed selling immensely, but he hated being put into a position in which he had to make decisions all day. As a result, he would put off those decisions. The more he looked at those decisions, the bigger they got, until he was overwhelmed. I shared with him an old saying: "If you must swallow a bullfrog, don't look at him too long, lest he become too big for you to swallow!"

All of us tend to procrastinate wherever we must make unpleasant choices. If we can change those situations, we owe it to ourselves—and to those around us—to change them. If we cannot change the unpleasant surroundings, we can best serve ourselves by doing what needs to be done as quickly, and as well, as we can.

WHY DO WE PROCRASTINATE?

"Man who waits for roast duck to fly into mouth must wait very, very long time," says an old Chinese proverb.

I've never met a person who liked putting things off, or the results of putting them off, but I've met a lot of people who do it. If we dislike it, and its effects, then why do so many of us do it so often?

Let's look beyond the flimsy excuses most of us offer to see if we can discover some of the real reasons behind our procrastination habits:

1. We kid ourselves into believing we'll have more time later. This tendency is especially true if the job we're putting off is a big one. But it also shows up in little things, like putting things back in their places when we have finished with them. Sooner or later, we have to face the consequences. And usually the task is bigger later than it would have been at the start.

2. They seem unimportant now. Maybe the results are too long-range for us to consider them important at the time. Perhaps we are so busy doing other things we have put off until they have become more urgent. Or sometimes we are simply not committed to them. Some people procrastinate so much that all they can do is run around like firefighters all day—putting out fires that should not have gotten started in the first place.

3. We are not pressed for completion. Many people are so undisciplined that, unless someone is pushing them to complete a task, they simply won't make it a priority. When they are pushed, they feel put upon.

4. We put off tasks because they seem unpleasant, difficult, or tedious. When we dread doing something, it's usually easier—for the moment—to come up with an excuse. Unfortunately, most of us find the dread to be counterproductive because the longer we dread the task, the worse it seems.

By far, the most common excuse is the last one: We dread doing something, so we put it off. All other excuses usually boil down to variations of these four reasons.

Simple mathematics can help us realize the folly of kidding ourselves about procrastination. Let's say we have a task that will probably take an hour to complete, and we put it off for two weeks. Most of us will worry, off and on, at least ten minutes each day about what we must do. Add a few minutes for the extra time it takes to do it because we have let it pile up. Total up the time worrying, the time added by delay, plus the original time required, and we have succeeded in turning a one-hour job into a three-and-a-half-hour job. But that's not the worst part of it. The emotional drain of worrying about it saps energy that we need to do other jobs we are attempting.

So why do we procrastinate? It becomes a habit.

HOW DO WE PROCRASTINATE?

Are you like the fellow who said, "I've decided a thousand times to quit putting things off, but I never got around to it"? The interesting thing about procrastination is that it has more to do with what we fail to do than with what we do. Usually, it means we simply fail to act on something we feel we should do. In fact, the way most of us procrastinate is to do nothing about something we should be doing something about. We wait for conditions to change, for a better opportunity, for the task to become more urgent. But mostly we wait until we feel more like doing it.

Remember, taking charge of your life means that you control your emotions, rather than allowing them to control you.

ARREST THE THIEF

We have called procrastination a nasty habit. Another name for a habit is a rut, which is nothing more than a grave with both ends knocked out of it! Putting things off has seldom been associated with winning. It's the losers who wait for things to happen. The winners in the game of life make things happen.

Of course, we're not talking about delaying an action for a valid reason. Some actions are best put off. For example, a campaign against procrastination once backfired. The manager of a large office decided too many things were being put off, so he posted a large sign in the office which said, "DO IT NOW!" The next week, the head bookkeeper absconded with $100,000, two junior executives turned in their notices and took jobs with competitors, the boss' secretary announced she was pregnant, and a clerk committed suicide.

Needless to say, the sign came down!

There are often legitimate reasons to postpone action. Waiting makes good sense—not procrastination—when you must have more information before you can take action, when an action would cause needless hurt to someone, or when conditions are simply not right. In those cases, waiting by design becomes positive action. Procrastination is the *unnecessary* delaying of a task that should be done immediately.

How Do You Arrest The Thief?

Here are some handcuffs you can use:

1. Get yourself organized and stay organized. Learn to schedule your tasks, set deadlines for yourself and others, and live by your schedules. Make appointments with yourself to start important projects at specific times, and keep those appointments faithfully.

2. Practice self-discipline. Make up your mind that you are going to adopt and live by the "do-it-now" attitude for every legitimate task.

3. Write down tasks that have been hanging too long and set a target date to begin and finish each. Set in motion a series of actions that will lead you to the habit of getting things done on schedule.

4. Learn to be decisive about tasks. Learn to decide whether or not a task is worth doing and act accordingly. If it is not worth doing, forget it—don't let it clutter your life. If it's worth doing, write it into your plans and do it!

If I may paraphrase Smokey the Bear, "Only you can help stamp out procrastination."

Go ahead . . . what are you waiting for?

Exercise 11–1. Arresting Procrastination

Make a list of at least five things you have been putting off until later, and set a target date to start and finish each:

1. Task _____ Start _____ Finish _____

2. Task _____ Start _____ Finish _____

3. Task _____ Start _____ Finish _____

4. Task _____ Start _____ Finish _____

5. Task _____ Start _____ Finish _____

chapter twelve
LEADERSHIP:
THE WINNER'S TASK

"Few people are successful unless a lot of other people want them to be," said Charlie Brower. How true that is! Whether you are a teacher, a lawyer, a salesperson, an artist, or an executive, your success in life depends in large measure on how well you are able to enlist the aid of other people in reaching your goals. Further, if you have written happiness into your plans for success, that happiness is strongly related to your ability to make sure that other people get something out of their relationships with you.

THREE KINDS OF PEOPLE

Someone has observed that there are basically three kinds of people:

1. Those who, when confronted with a situation, can determine what needs to be done, come up with a way of doing it, and get it done.
2. Those who, when confronted with a situation and shown what needs to be done, can come up with a way of doing it and get it done.
3. Those who, when confronted with a situation and shown what needs to be done and how to do it, can get the job done.

Which kind of person are you? Are you a "take-charge" person who can, when faced with a situation, decide what needs to be done, figure out how to do it, and then get it done?

Leaders Are Made, Not Born

Some people seem to be effective leaders with what appears to be a minimum of preparation and effort. They seem to possess a certain innate magical ingredient that we often refer to as "charisma." However, if you study the careers of the truly great leaders of history, you find that their "charisma" grew more from what they did than from some mysterious quality they possessed.

Napoleon, for example, is often thought of as a great military strategist and a strong personality. Yet Napoleon said that the secret of his success lay in his ability to arouse men to action by the techniques he utilized. The same can be said for the Lincolns, the Roosevelts, the Kennedys, and many others.

Remember, what you are and hope to be is the way you experience yourself, but other people experience you by what you do. What you do leads other people to join in and to help you to reach your goals.

PRINCIPLES OF LEADERSHIP

Every person is different. Every leadership situation is different. And every task is different. What works for one person, in one situation or in the completion of one task, might not work with others. However, certain underlying principles, employed by the great leaders of history, can help us become more effective leaders.

PRINCIPLE 1
Understand the People You Would Lead

The most fundamental principle of leading other people is to *understand the people you would lead*! Desire is the key to any form of discipline or attempt at motivation. "If you would be successful as a leader," someone said, "discover what people want, and help them achieve it." Your success comes when you are helping other people achieve what is important to them.

Charles Percy was made president of Bell & Howell, Inc. before he was forty years old. A business news reporter, fascinated by his rapid rise to such a responsible position, asked many people to what they attributed Percy's success. "From the very beginning," the answer always came back, "he showed a knack for being able to get the most out of other people." This sensitivity to the needs and desires of other people ultimately led him to national prominence as a U.S. Senator.

Whether your task is to sell or market products, to lead people to produce goods or services, or to help people change their lives, the principle is the same—know and understand those you would lead. Perhaps this requirement is why so many successful leaders are such avid students of human nature. Perhaps this is why they are fascinated by subjects like psychology, sociology, philosophy, and religion. They want to understand why people act the way they do. "We don't want geniuses for managers," says a well-known company president, "We want people who can motivate other people to do good work."

Much has been said in recent years about the increasing role of the computer in business and our world in general. Many even fear that computers will take over the leadership of this world. I believe computers will never be able to assert strong leadership over people for one simple reason—they simply don't have the capacity to understand human nature. Computers lack the ability to comprehend the illogic of human emotions, the capacities of people to love, to desire, and to fear, or the qualitative dimensions of a person's work habits.

For example, one person tries to get by with as little effort as possible, to turn out sloppy work and get away with it, or to cover up mistakes, Yet another person becomes a "workaholic," strives for excellence, and corrects his or her own mistakes. A computer can report the end result. It may even collect enough data to determine what best motivates people in a given situation. But it takes the sensitivity of the human mind to understand why certain people react as they do, to spot the potential for better performance by changing the situations in which people work, and to lead people toward better performance.

There will always be room in the workplace, and in the area of human services, for leaders who can spot the strengths and weaknesses of an individual for a particular task, and either structure that task to build on those strengths or find another task that will be more suitable. By the same token, a computer in a mass-production facility would blow a circuit trying to find a place for a person like Antonio Stradivari who said, "Other men will make other violins, but none shall make a better one." To this day, the violins he made bring from $15,000 to $500,000.

But a sensitive leader would not try to fit a man like Stradivari into a production line. Instead, that leader would utilize his talents in designing prototypes or in making special violins for a very limited and discriminating market.

Whatever else you may learn about leadership, nothing will ever make you more effective than a genuine and sincere interest in those people you would lead, along with a keen understanding of their strengths and weaknesses. The "big stick" approach to leadership went out with the dark ages. If leaders try to operate in today's complex world with the notion that "the boss may not always be right, but he's always the boss," they will find most of those they would lead "marching to the beat of a different drummer." The self-centered individual gets frustrated by the weaknesses of others and by their apparent lack of motivation to do the tasks to which they are assigned, but the creative leader looks for ways of capitalizing on their strengths and desires.

PRINCIPLE 2
Master the Basic Tasks of Leadership

Of basically three types of leadership, each has its place.

"Autocratic" Leadership. This type of leader maintains tight control of the group, holds few meetings, and barks out orders. A fire chief, coming to the scene of a major hotel fire, might illustrate the best of "autocratic" leadership. It would be foolish for the chief to call a meeting of all the firefighters to try to decide what they should do first. You would most likely hear orders like: "Move unit one to location X! . . . Bring that hose over here! . . . Take three men and go in there!" At least, if I were in that burning hotel, that's what I would hope the chief would do!

"Democratic" Leadership. The leader calls meetings and asks for input from various people, then allows the group to decide what should be done. For example, after a fire, that same fire chief might meet with the department heads to critique how well the depart-

ment handled the situation and how they could be more effective in future fires.

"Free-Rein" Leadership. Here the emphasis is on loose control and maximum participation. The leader leads the group to explore and adopt solutions to problems. Again, the fire chief might well call a meeting of all the people in the fire department to participate in a "brainstorming" session to collect ideas as to how future fires could be prevented.

People who lead successfully know how to determine which type of leadership each situation needs, and they seek to adapt their styles of leadership to those situations.

Regardless of the leadership style called for, the leader must perform five basic tasks or operations. Master each of them, and you can become an effective leader.

Task 1: Set Goals and Objectives

As a leader, you must set goals and objectives for those you would lead. This involves knowing what needs to be done and how to get it done. Just as in your personal goal-setting function, you need to provide purpose and direction for the people you would lead. This task might sound simple, but it can often become very complex. If we may go back to the fire chief for illustration, the chief must set priorities for all of the resources available.

The effective leader knows how to assess a situation, set priorities, and establish goals. The obvious goal is to put out the fire. However, if you happened to be in the hotel, you would probably hope that the fire chief would place saving lives above putting out the fire. Goals for coping with the fire might be: (1) Minimize the danger to human life, (2) contain the flames, smoke, and fumes, (3) protect as yet undamaged property, and (4) put out the fire.

Task 2: Plan and Organize

If you would lead, you must learn how to plan and to organize the available resources to tackle the challenge at hand. This task includes analyzing what decisions need to be made and by whom, dividing the work into manageable tasks, and selecting the people to do the jobs called for. It includes such questions as:

- What activities need to be carried out?
- What resources are needed to perform those activities?
- How can the people and other resources available be used to maximum advantage?
- What specific contribution can each available person be realistically expected to make?

Our overworked fire chief is likely to be very ineffective at fighting a major fire unless he has done some advance planning. For example, in meeting the priority of saving lives, he needs a team of specially trained, specially equipped, and properly supervised people to go to the rescue of those in peril. That team also needs a wide variety of backup systems to help them carry out their task.

Task 3: Communicate and Motivate People

The leader communicates what is to be done, who is to do it, and how it is to be done. Then comes the task of motivating people to do it. By effectively communicating and stimulating people to act, the leader pulls the individuals together into a team. Each person's task is designed to contribute to the progress of the team as a whole. Those who are led must be made to understand the overall objectives of the group, along with the role each of them must play to enable the group to meet those objectives.

The burden of communicating always rests primarily on the shoulders of the leader. In many ways, this task is often the toughest for the person who would lead. Management experts say that nearly 80 percent of the failures of organizations to reach their goals can be traced to a breakdown in communications. In other words, people who fail to carry out their assigned tasks most often do so because they don't understand what is expected of them. If someone fails, it is usually unproductive to upbraid the person because he or she didn't understand.

Returning to our example, a team leader who doesn't understand that role might desert his post and try to play the hero in rescuing an individual. His failure might well jeopardize the lives of several of his team members and hamper efforts to rescue many other people in peril.

Like the skilled and sensitive conductor, the able leader orchestrates the talents and motivations of the individuals in the group to produce the harmony of teamwork.

Task 4: Measure Performance

The leader measures performance. That everybody is busy "doing something" is not enough. Each person must be contributing what is expected in relation to the overall task. This process is the responsibility of the leader. This task involves deciding how and with what yardsticks performance will be measured, making every person aware of the criteria by which he or she will be measured, and relating the performance of each individual to the overall goals and objectives that have been set.

Task 5: Develop People

Finally, leaders develop people—including themselves. Effective leaders know that every person in the organization must grow and learn constantly. Farsighted leaders know that tomorrow will be another day, presenting challenges and opportunities that are even greater than those of today. So such leaders cultivate the available talent to keep expanding horizons. More than that, perceptive leaders know that people perform better in their present situations when they see themselves as learning, expanding their horizons, and growing. Developing people is a constant process for the effective leader.

PRINCIPLE 3
Master Basic Tools and Skills of Leadership

The leader can use certain basic tools and skills to become more effective at getting people to do things. Let's look at these tools:

Tool 1:
Workable, Reasonable Objectives

When people are told to do something in a general way and when they get the time, that's usually the way it gets done—if it gets done. Effective managers not only set goals and objectives for themselves; they set goals and objectives for all they seek to lead. And they take it one step further: They involve those to be led in the goal-setting process and encourage them to set objectives for themselves. A well run organization places constant emphasis on planning—from the top down to the lowest level of activity. When people are involved in the process of setting goals and objectives, they are more apt to be supportive of the leader's efforts to get things done on schedule.

In addition, people who are actually responsible for carrying out objectives can often give valuable input. For example, Henry Ford often said that when he had a time-consuming and unpleasant task to do, he would assign the "laziest man I can find" to do the job. "Within a day or two, he will come up with a quick and easy way to do it," he observed.

Workable, reasonable objectives for all people in the organization are an effective tool of leadership.

Tool 2
Effective Monitoring Techniques

Often a leader, despite a "gut-level feeling" that an organization or a group of people is not living up to its potential, can't seem to put a finger on just why. Usually, the reason is that there are not adequate systems for monitoring the progress of individuals and units toward the objectives that have been set. The effective leader knows what each person is doing, in relation both to his or her capabilities and to the objectives that have been set for them.

Simple time-management techniques can help to increase the efficiency of each person in an organization in several ways. First, they can make the person aware that time is important. Second, they can give the person a goal. Third, when carefully monitored, they can provide the basis for rewards and reproofs.

Performance standards can be used to increase the effectiveness of all people who are contributing to the objectives. Some of the tools leader use to monitor performance are:

1. *Measurement of accomplishment of the assigned task*: This tool includes such things as production quotas, work schedules, and deadlines.

2. *Measurement of activities*: Allowance must be made of assigned jobs that do not relate directly to the accomplishment of the leader's goals but that are important to the overall operation.

3. *Qualitative and intangible measurements*: These would include customer goodwill, planning and organizing abilities, imagination and creativity, ambition, appearance, and knowledge of the company and its products.

Tool 3
Productive Meetings

In a scene from the movie *Ben Hur*, Judah Ben Hur was trying to get a team of horses to pull a chariot. They were magnificent, high-spirited animals—yet they were pawing the ground, balking at his commands, and scarcely moving the chariot, despite his strong voice and the constant cracking of his whip. A skilled old horse trainer approached and instantly put his finger on the problem. "They are not pulling together as a team!" he told young Judah Ben Hur. The old man adjusted the rig, carefully aligned the horses, and climbed into the chariot. He cracked his whip and instantly— four horses started as one. Around the track they went at breath-taking speeds.

"They are beautiful babies," said the old man as he handed the reins back to Judah, "But you must make them work together as a team."

That is a good scene to keep in mind each time you are called upon to lead a meeting. As a leader and motivator of people, you will probably be called upon many times to conduct meetings. The success or failure of those meetings depends largely on how effective you are as a chairperson. Often the mindpower assembled in a room is awesome, but it is up to you, the leader, to get all of those minds to work together as a team.

Good meetings don't just happen! They are the result of the skill-ful use of certain basic ingredients:

1. Careful planning and preparation before the meeting.
2. Strong leadership at the meeting.
3. Proper handling of distractions.
4. Effective follow-up.

Leading meetings can be one of the most challenging and exciting activities of your career and community life. Those who do it well experience the rewards of leading others to fulfillment and meaningful activity.

Tool 4
Effective Communication

Experts say that at least 80 percent of what a leader does can be summed up in one word—communication! So important is this tool of leadership that we devote an entire chapter to it later. At this point, however, we must understand its role as one of the most vital tools of leadership.

Every time I speak at a convention in San Francisco, I go for a ride on the Golden Gate bridge. I have always been awed by this enormous and magnificent structure, which serves a useful and vital function. To be sure, the bridge is a masterpiece of design and engineering. Perhaps even more amazing, the materials and manpower needed to build it were actually assembled and coordinated by human beings. Just think, for a moment, of all the people it took to build that tremendous masterpiece: architects, engineers, steelworkers, concrete workers, plumbers, electricians, and so on. Drawing on the resources necessary to complete that structure, within a reasonably short time, has to be considered a monument to effective communication.

If an area of leadership calls for the best use of a person's talents above all the others, it is the area of effective communication. Leaders who know how to communicate their goals and objectives, in a manner that leads to their fulfillment, will always be much in demand.

Tool 5
Good Human Relations

The person who would lead others must master good human relations as a tool of effective leadership. Good leaders are often very demanding. They expect the best from those around them, and they usually get it. But they get it by realizing that they are leaders of free people—not drivers of slaves!

Here are a few rules of good human relations:

1. *Value people.* "Anyone can be polite to a king," someone has observed, "but it takes a gentleman to be polite to a beggar." If what Charlie Brower says is true—if our success depends on how many people want us to be successful—then it follows that people really do matter to us. Sincere gratitude for people's contributions to the achievement of your goals can be one of the most valuable attitudes you'll ever cultivate.

2. *Be an active listener.* Someone has wisely observed that the greatest compliment you can pay people is to listen to them. People give more fully of themselves to leaders who genuinely seek to understand their needs, concerns, and desires.

3. *Be tactful.* Criticize only constructively, and then only sparingly. When it is necessary to criticize, make sure you do it in private and that you criticize actions rather than persons. John Wanamaker, one of the all-time great business leaders said, "Whatever you have to say to people be sure to say it in words that will cause them to smile and you will be on pretty safe ground." Then, he offered this sage advice: "And when you do find it necessary to criticize someone, put your criticism in the form of a question which the other fellow is practically sure to have to answer in a manner that he becomes his own critic."

Common courtesy can be a valuable tool of leadership.

4. *Give—don't seek—credit.* Some leaders constantly fail because they seek to blame others for mistakes and to take credit for achievements. The wise leader praises—in public—each person who contributes something to the overall task. Giving credit is a great investment: it costs nothing and pays big dividends in human relations.

5. *Be consistent.* Effective leaders learn to control their moods. They don't praise someone for an action because they feel good one day, and criticize them for the same action the next day just because they feel badly. They also treat all people similarly. They don't play favorites.

6. *Be willing to lose face.* When you make a mistake, be willing to admit that mistake. As an erring human, you're in pretty good

company. Henry Ford forgot to put a reverse gear in his first car. Edison once spent more than $2 million on an invention that proved useless.

Great leaders are not afraid to admit their mistakes. Samuel Johnson spent years compiling the first significant English dictionary. Along the way, he made a few goofs, like identifying the "pastern" as the knee of a horse, when any person of learning should know it is part of the hoof.

"How could you make such a mistake," a critic assailed.

"Ignorance, madam! Pure ignorance!" said Johnson, and the subject was promptly dropped.

Leaders who readily admit their mistakes, find that they gain, rather than lose, the respect of those around them by their willingness to lose face.

7. *Cultivate a good sense of humor*. A pleasant, approachable manner can go a long way toward building a good work atmosphere. Of course, the workplace is no place for excess joking, storytelling, and frivolity, but an occasional laugh can ease the tension of a busy group of people. "A good sense of humor helps to overlook the unbecoming, understand the unconventional, tolerate the unpleasant, overcome the unexpected, and outlast the unbearable," someone said.

8. *Set a good example*. Nothing breeds loyalty in a group of people any more effectively than loyalty by the leader. The same is true of integrity, punctuality, respect for deadlines, creativity, and many other desirable traits. The chairman of the board of a large corporation punches a clock—and insists that every executive on his staff do the same thing. "If we must require it of our employees," he says, "why shouldn't we do it ourselves?"

PRINCIPLE 4
Master the Art of Negotiating

Franklin D. Roosevelt said, "It has always seemed to me that the best symbol of common sense was the bridge." If you would be a successful leader, you must learn to creatively build bridges in all of your relationships with other people. For example, two boys were squabbling over a small piece of pie. After much heated debate over who would get the larger slice, the two approached their father, who had heard their loud and emotional debates. They asked him to settle the dispute.

"Why don't you cut the piece of pie into two equal slices? That way each of you would get half," he suggested.

"No way!" each of the boys shouted.

The father then proposed a creative solution. "Flip a coin to see which of you will cut the pie. The other one then will be allowed to choose which piece he wants to take."

The boys agreed, flipped a coin, and the pie was cut. Interestingly, the piece was cut into two exactly equal slices. That's a very good example of creatively building bridges. The process is sometimes called "negotiating."

Whether we are closing a sale, buying a house, applying for a job, supervising a worker, or proposing marriage—all of us are negotiating constantly. Negotiating ranges all the way from settling a dispute between two boys over a piece of pie, to Strategic Arms Limitation Talks between two superpowers to reduce the threat of nuclear war. The art of negotiating is based on a simple fact—all of us need the cooperation of other people if we are to reach our career and personal goals. And each of us brings to life's bargaining table something that others value.

Leaders who master the art of negotiating are usually the most successful. Successful leaders gain the cooperation they need to reach their goals by building bridges to agreements in which everybody wins.

Perceptive leaders know that people can be forced into submission only up to a certain point—and then only for a short time. Someone said that "even the lowly rat, when cornered, will turn and fight." Effective leaders want not only productivity from those around them, but also loyalty, integrity, commitment, creativity, and enthusiasm. Those intangibles can only come about through their use of the art of give and take.

If you would be a successful leader, learn the art of negotiating. Here are some pointers that can help:

Pointer 1:
People Do Things for Their Reasons, Not Yours

Offer a new idea and people want to know, "What's in it for me?" Announce a new personnel policy and people ask, "What's in it for me?" Effective leaders understand this need and see to it that everyone in every negotiating situation comes away with some benefit. Thus people are willing to support their actions enthusiastically.

Pointer 2:
Gain Cooperation by Satisfying the Needs of People

The sound of one hand clapping is only *silence*. Successful leaders know that they need the support of those people around them if they are to meet their goals. The most successful leaders gain that support by helping other people to meet their needs.

Professor Maslow defines the basic needs that all humans bring to life's bargaining table as follows:

1. People have *physiological* needs—like food, clothing, and shelter. They are expressed as "I want to live."
2. People have needs of *security* and *safety*—"I want to be protected; I want to live tomorrow."
3. People have a need for *social belonging*—they want to be loved.
4. People have a need for *self-esteem*—they want to be important.
5. People have a need for *self-fulfillment*—they want to contribute something worthwhile.
6. People need to *know and understand*—they want to learn and grow.
7. Finally, people have *aesthetic needs*—they want to make their lives pleasant and their surroundings attractive.

If you help people to satisfy these basic needs, you can gain their enthusiastic support and cooperation. By helping others meet their needs, you can obtain your goals.

Pointer 3
Seek Balance in the Negotiating Process

Good leaders are often very demanding. They give freely of themselves and their resources—and they expect others to respond by giving freely. It works!

- When you give loyalty, you have a right to expect loyalty in return.
- When you give integrity, you have a right to expect others to give you integrity.
- When you are sensitive to the needs of others, you have every right to expect them to be sensitive to your needs and goals.

Remember, the effective leader—the master bridge builder—makes sure that everybody comes away from every give-and-take situation with *something*. Effective negotiators make sure that everybody—including themselves—wins!

As a leader, you are not seeking total surrender. You are seeking a balanced solution to each conflict, a mutually beneficial agreement in each negotiation, and a cooperative climate in which each person's needs and goals can be met.

If you would be a successful leader, you must learn to creatively build bridges in all of your relationships.

PRINCIPLE 5
Learn to Use the Basic Motivators

If assuming that you can motivate anyone is a mistake, then equally foolish is the assumption that some people are unmotivated. Some people might not do what you, as a leader, would like them to do, but it is not due to a lack of motivation. It is rather because they are motivated to do something else.

When leaders understand that people have certain basic motivations, and that people respond to appeals to those motivations, they can be very successful at getting people to do things. Napoleon, for example, could get his troops to accomplish feats that many people would consider impossible because he understood what motivates people and he used the basic motivators. He first determined what his men wanted most, then did all in his power to help them get it. When his army was weak from hunger, he told them that the way to get food was to take it from the enemy by defeating them. When most of his army was homesick, and many were thinking of deserting, he made his appeal to their pride by asking them how they wanted to return home—as conquering heroes or as cowards who ran from the enemy? While fighting among the pyramids of Egypt, he called forth their sense of history and told them: "Forty centuries are looking down on you."

The leader's task, then, is to create an environment that is conducive to self-motivation. Certain basic motivators can be used to good advantage by the effective leader:

1. Achievement. People basically want to achieve. Looking at some people, you might find that statement hard to believe, but it's true. They may not want to achieve what you want them to achieve, but they want to achieve.

A wise father was once faced with a boy who wouldn't study in school and who was constantly causing disruptions. Noticing that the boy enjoyed working on small motors, he helped him set up a repair shop in the family garage. By giving the boy the responsibility for keeping his own books, he used the interest in motors to stimulate the boy to study mathematics. Soon, the boy was doing well in mathematics—his worst subject. Gradually, the boy's sense of achievement spread into other areas, and soon the boy was doing well in other subjects. By the time he graduated, he had a thriving business.

The effective leader looks for ways to give people an opportunity to achieve what is important to them, in a manner that will accomplish his or her goals.

2. Recognition. People want to be recognized for the contributions they make. The form of the recognition—a raise, a pat on the back, or a public commendation—is not nearly as crucial as the fact that the recognition is given regularly and consistently. Behaviorists call it positive reinforcement. When people are recognized for what they do, they usually try harder.

3. Participation. People are social creatures. They want to be a part of the action. And they want to be a part of the decision-making process. Most people want their opinions to be heard, and they want decisions affecting their work environment and tasks to be made only after they have been consulted.

4. Growth. People want an opportunity to grow, to learn to develop their abilities. Boredom is one of the biggest problems facing the average worker in America today. They have been locked into jobs that provide little opportunity to learn. They are expected to do the same thing day after day. Effective leaders can help people deal with the problem of boredom and make them productive by creatively structuring job-related growth opportunities.

When you understand and utilize these basic motivators, you will find them to be very helpful in leading other people to accomplish your goals.

A LOOK BACK

Someone has said that 10 percent of the people in America are responsible for initiating 90 percent of the productive action that takes place. That means that approximately 90 percent of the people are content to follow where others lead.

There will always be a valuable place in our society for those people who can effectively lead others. When you have mastered the principles outlined in this chapter, you are well on your way to becoming an effective leader.

chapter thirteen
EFFECTIVE COMMUNICATIONS MAKE THINGS HAPPEN

Through high-technology electronics, our world has become more interconnected than ever in man's history. A volcano eruption in Washington, martial law in Poland, or an assassination attempt on the life of our president . . . news of events reaches us within a matter of minutes; often from the other side of the world. Yet, even with all but instant communication, we constantly hear stories about people dying—while screaming for help—because nobody heard their cries.

- Peter Drucker claims that 60 percent of all management problems result from faulty communications.
- A leading marriage counsellor says that at least half of the divorces in this country can be traced to faulty communication between spouses.
- Many laws and government regulations fail to achieve their purpose, and sometimes produce the opposite of the intended effect, because their meanings are misunderstood.

What's the problem? Lack of communication? Certainly not! *If anything, we overcommunicate*! The problem stems from our failure to communicate *effectively*!

Someone has defined communication as a "meeting of meanings." The word communication comes from a latin word meaning "to make common." It sounds simple. Yet consider this "communication problem": "I know you think you understand what I said, but I'm not sure that what you thought you understood was what I thought I meant."

137

Part of the problem stems from the use of words themselves. The 500 most common words in the English language have 14,000 meanings, for an average of 28 meanings per word. To further complicate things, those meanings constantly change—from time to time and from person to person. In addition, with more than 700,000 kinds of nonverbal communication, the exchange of information and ideas becomes an even more complex process. As if that were not enough, many messages are poorly sent, and many more are poorly received. Thus we say things we don't mean, and understand things others do not mean.

EFFECTIVE COMMUNICATION— THE MASTER KEY TO SUCCESS

If you would be successful, both in your career and in all your personal relationships, you must communicate effectively. How do you communicate effectively? Let me illustrate.

A man and a woman are walking on a beach on a moonlit night. They pause for a moment and look deeply into each other's eyes.

"I love you!" he says.

"I love you, too," she replies.

"Will you marry me?" he asks.

"Yes!" she answers.

Hand in hand, the two walk on down the beach.

Four simple sentences were spoken, but those short sentences will change the lives of two people, and perhaps of others, *forever*! Let's break the dialog down to see how it was effective communication.

1. He conveyed a *message* in a way that it could be *understood* by the person to whom he was speaking.
2. She *accepted* his expression of love.
3. She *responded* with her *own* expression of love.
4. Each understood the *meaning* that the other sought to convey.

That was only the *first* exchange of information and opinion. Yet it was so effective that it opened the door to the *second* exchange, which went like this:

1. He asked a question or made a request, which she *understood*.
2. She *accepted* him, and his request.
3. She *responded positively*—she granted his request.
4. Each person came away with a *clearer understanding* of the other.

As simple as that little illustration is, it contains the power to enable you to communicate effectively through any medium, with any audience, to convey any message. That's a big claim, but let's break it down to see how it works.

Being Understood

How many times have you heard someone exclaim, "I've told you that a thousand times!"? The sad fact is that such a person might say "that" a thousand more times and still not have it understood. The goal of effective communication is to convey a message in a way that it is *received* and *understood*.

For example, two men made speeches in a little Pennsylvania town one day more than a century ago. One was a professional orator who made an outstanding speech. His words have long been forgotten. The other man was a simple, awkward man who violated all the rules of public speaking. Yet after more than 100 years, Lincoln's Gettysburg Address is one of the most often quoted speeches of all history. What made that simple little speech a classic of effective communication?

It Was:
The right person
 Saying the right thing
  To the right people
   At the right time
    In the right place
     In the right way

And It Was:
Heard correctly
 Understood
  Received

Thus It Produced:
The desired response.

These ingredients of being understood are so basic that most of us tend to forget them. If you would have your messages understood, learn and stick to the basics.

Your Goal Is to Be Accepted!

You want people to agree with you—or at least give you a sympathetic hearing. Here are ten suggestions to help you be accepted:

1. Be natural, be yourself, be real.
2. Set a conducive atmosphere.
3. Always look your best.
4. Establish your authority to speak to a subject.
5. Organize what you want to say—don't ramble.
6. Speak to needs—use words that have meaning to your audience.
7. Involve your audience.
8. Be enthusiastic—keep your voice lively.
9. Be humorous—remember, "A spoonful of sugar helps the medicine go down."
10. Use visual aids—people remember more of what they see than what they hear.

You Want to Produce the Desired Response

If you want to get something done, be certain that you get the response you desire. As an illustration, a very shy young man once wanted to win the affection of a lady. Once a day, for a whole year, he sent her a postcard, telling her of his love for her. His plan was to ask her to marry him at the end of that year. Sure enough, she got married at the end of the year—to the postman. He got action, but not the response he desired! If you would get people to do what you want them to do, you must seek to convince them that it is in their best interest to act as you suggest.

"Never make your appeal to a man's better nature; he may not have one," said Lazarus Long, the wise old prophet of science fiction. "Always make your appeal to his self interest." People who understand this principle don't try to get action by demanding or ordering others to do things. They don't beg, and they don't threaten. Instead they are effective communicators because they have learned the power of persuasion. If you would be an effective communicator, learn how to get things done through persuasion.

Understanding Others

The cycle of communication is complete *only* when you come away with a clearer understanding of the person or persons with whom you sought to communicate. Many sales, for example, are lost because the salesperson pays little attention to the messages the client is sending back. A young salesman went into a house to sell books. He made a masterful demonstration of his products, and the lady who had invited him in was very cordial. Finally he came to the close. He used an alternate close—right out of the sales manual. No sale. Later, as the young salesman explained his frustration to his sales manager, he asked where he might have gone wrong.

"I set up that presentation to teach you a very important lesson," replied the sales manager, with a smile, "You see, that woman is blind and has no need for your books."

The embarrassed young salesman never forgot that lesson. He learned the value of feedback. Effective communication is always a two-way street. Drive down that street the wrong way, and you are headed for a collision with your audience.

Remember, the goals of effective communication are:

- Being understood
- Being accepted
- Getting the desired response
- And understanding others

ARE YOU REALLY LISTENING?

The person who would learn to communicate effectively must first learn to listen effectively. Someone said that most problems in relationships boil down to a failure on the part of one or more persons to listen actively to what is being said. This is true whether we are talking about our mates, our customers, or the people we work with everyday. "Many people know how to talk, but few know how to listen," is the way the president of Xerox Corporation recently assessed the problem. His company has launched a major program to help people in all industries learn how to listen. In actuality, most people's form of communication is a "monolog in duet." In other words, "You think up what you are going to say while he says what he thought up while you were talking."

Active listening could solve many of our most serious problems; it could enable us to work more productively and happily. In a book called *The Miracle of Dialog*, Dr. Reuel Howe talks about two-way communication. He says that to dialog is to "get into significant touch with another person." Many people have never discovered the tremendous benefits of active listening, or getting into significant touch with others. I'd like to list a few of those benefits of active listening. I hope you are listening.

Benefit 1
We Can Learn

Emerson said, "Every man I meet is in some way my superior, and, in that, I can learn of him." I have never met a person from whom I could not learn something—if I took the time and trouble to actively listen.

Benefit 2
We Express Interest in
the Person to Whom We Listen

By actively listening, we can affirm that other persons have value to us, that they matter, that they have worth as human beings. Active listeners care about people—and people know that they do.

Benefit 3
We Gain Insight Into the
Needs, Desires, and Motivations of Others

During the great depression, a young man went to a telegraph office to apply for a job. As he walked into the lobby, he noticed that many other people—some even sitting on the floor—were filling out applications. He sat down, but only for a moment, and then jumped to his feet and walked into the inner office.

A few moments later the receptionist announced that the position had been filled.

"Why did that man get the job?" complained several of the other applicants. "He came in after we did!".

The answer was simple! While the others sat filling out applications, the young man *listened*. Someone in the inner office was tapping out the following message in Morse code: "We need an operator. If you understand this message, the job is yours. Please come in." While the others were busy telling the prospective employer about *themselves*, that young man was *listening* to the needs of the *prospective employer*.

Benefit 4
We Break Down Barriers

Due to the "natural" barriers, people tune us out. By actively listening, we can break down such barriers as differences in language and our understanding of words, prejudices, anxiety-produced defenses, and conflicts over perceived differences in our goals and theirs. As such barriers drop, others hear us.

Benefit 5
We Involve Others in the
Process We Want to Take Place

Whether you are trying to win the affection of a lover, sell a ten-story building, or talk a police officer out of a parking ticket, you will not succeed *unless* the person to whom you are talking becomes involved in the conversation. You may not succeed anyway, but you have a much better chance if the person is actively involved in the process through your active listening.

Benefit 6
We Can Clarify Misconceptions

Often we reject what people are saying, because we misunderstand what they mean. These explanations of how accidents occurred, taken from actual insurance forms, can illustrate the problem of taking what people say literally:

- "The telephone pole was approaching fast, I was attempting to swerve out of its path when it struck my front end." Those poles can chase you down!
- "I had been driving my car for four years when I fell asleep at the wheel and had an accident." That's got to be a record!

- "I was on my way to the doctor's with rear end trouble when my universal joint gave way causing me to have an accident." Really? What kind of doctor?
- "To avoid hitting the bumper of the car in front, I struck the pedestrian."

Sometimes it takes a lot of active listening to hear what people are trying to tell us. The other side of the coin is that people reject what we say because we don't adequately convey what we mean. Sometimes we can be as clumsy as the fellow who was trying to compliment his hostess.

"Your daughter is beautiful," he said (and should have quit). "She's even prettier than you!"

Realizing how that must have sounded, he quickly attempted a recovery.

"That's not what I meant," he stumbled, "Actually, she's not pretty at all."

Unfortunately, many of the misconceptions that make it hard for us to communicate effectively are not so humorous. Sometimes they can cause loss, pain, and grief. Only when we actively listen can we hear and clear up misconceptions.

HOW DO YOU ACTIVELY LISTEN?

1. Be open! Switch off all negative thoughts about the person. Be receptive to what is being said. Drop those emotional barriers that filter out what is being said or that cause you to hear only what you want to hear.

2. Start listening with the first sentence! Self-centered people can't actively listen. They tend to be preoccupied with their own daydreams. Put aside what you are doing, and concentrate on what the person is saying.

3. Concentrate on what is being said. Actively try to hear every word as if it were the most important thing you could hear at that moment. Avoid the temptation to think faster than the person is talking.

4. Look for the meaning of what is being said. Don't try to read your own meanings into what the person is saying. Rather, help the person convey his or her own meanings by showing genuine interest.

5. Avoid the temptation to interrupt. As Dr. David Schwartz, in his book *The Magic of Thinking Big*, says, "Big people monopolize the listening. Small people monopolize the talking."

6. Ask questions that stimulate the person to talk, and clarify your understanding of what is being said. To test your understanding, use trial questions, like "Do I understand correctly that . . ."

7. File away important points being made. If appropriate, take notes.

8. Screen out interruptions and ignore distractions.

9. Use facial expressions and body language to express interest and comprehension.

10. Don't over-react to highly charged or emotional words. Look for the meanings behind those words. Avoid jumping to conclusions. Hear the person out.

MASTER THE ART OF LISTENING

The more effectively you listen, the more you will learn. When the late President Lyndon B. Johnson was a junior senator from Texas, he kept a sign on his office wall that read, "You ain't learnin' nothin' when you're doin' all the talkin'." But, perhaps equally important, the more you are willing to listen to others, the better you will become at communicating.

A LOOK BACK

Communication with other human beings is, at best, a complex and confusing task, but is is usually worth every effort we put into it. Through effective communications we exchange information, ideas, and opinions with other people, we integrate our lives into the human race, and we make happen the things we want to happen. If you would be successful, both in your career and in all your personal relationships, you must learn to communicate effectively. Through effective communications, you can be understood, you can have your messages accepted, you can produce the responses you desire, and you can emerge with a clearer understanding between you and the other people. But the person who would learn to communicate effectively must first learn how to listen effectively.

Remember, the goal of communication is to get "into significant touch with another person." That is always worth the effort.

Exercise 13–1. Elements of Effective Communication

The four elements of effective communication are (1) being understood, (2) being accepted, (3) producing a desired response, and (4) understanding others. As you review each of the four elements, apply it by doing the exercise that follows it.

Being Understood
The goal of effective communication is to convey a message in a way that it is received and understood.

APPLICATION EXERCISE: Think of a message you tried to send that was not received and/or understood. Describe how you might have sent it to obtain the desired effect:

_____

_____

_____

Being Accepted
You want people to agree with you—or at least to give your message a sympathetic hearing.

APPLICATION EXERCISE: Think of a message you sent recently that gained a sympathetic hearing. Why was it accepted?

_____

_____

_____

Producing the Desired Response
When you communicate, you want action. You want the people who hear you to do something in response.

APPLICATION EXERCISE: You wanted something done. They understood and accepted your message. Yet they did not do it.

Why?

_____

_____

What might you have done that would have changed the outcome?

_____

_____

Understanding Others
Effective communications lead to a better understanding of other people.

APPLICATION EXERCISE: Analyze a recent successful communications effort from which you felt you understood better the person involved. What insights did you gain from the communication?

_____

_____

_____

How might you have gained a deeper understanding of the person?

_____

_____

Exercise 13–1 (*cont.*)

How Good a Listener Are You?

If you would be an effective communicator, you must first learn to be an active listener. Here's a little self-evaluation exercise to help you pin down just how good you are at listening. Rate yourself, on a scale of 1–5, on each statement:

1. I enjoy listening to people talk.

2. I encourage other people to talk.

3. I listen, even when I do not particularly like the person talking.

4. The sex of the person talking makes no difference in how well I listen.

5. I listen equally well to a friend, an acquaintance, or a stranger.

6. I put away what I am doing while someone is talking.

7. I look at the person talking.

8. I ignore distractions while listening to a person talk.

9. I smile, nod my head, and otherwise encourage the person to talk.

10. I concentrate on what the person is saying.

11. I try to understand what the person means.

12. I seek to understand why the person is saying it.

13. I never interrupt the person talking.

14. If the person hesitates, I encourage him/her to continue.

15. I restate what the person has said and ask if I got it right.

16. I withhold all judgments about the person's idea or message until I have heard all the person has to say about it.

17. I listen regardless of the person's tone of voice, attitude, or choice of words.

18. I don't anticipate what the person is going to say—just listen.

19. I ask questions to get ideas explained more fully.

20. I ask for clarification of words I do not understand in their context.

Add Up the Point Value of Your Ratings and Score Yourself as Follows:

86–100 You're all ears.

71–85 You're a pretty good listener.

56–70 You're missing a lot.

55 and under It might be a good idea to have your ears checked.

chapter fourteen
HOW TO HANDLE STRESS AND DISTRESS

Let's face it: Anyone who is expecting life to be all fun and games is living in an impractical dreamland! Sometimes life gets tough, real tough. And it seems that the farther up the ladder of success you climb, the tougher life gets. Someone defined the boss as a person who worked hard eight hours a day, five days a week, to get into a position where he could work even harder—twelve hours a day, seven days a week.

A popular sign reads, "It's mine, I worked for it, I deserve it! And as soon as I have time, I'll have my nervous breakdown!" That's a humorous way of talking about something that, for many people, is a serious problem. It's probably a good thing that we can joke about stress. Otherwise, just talking about it might lead us to distress. Stress is one of the most talked-about, yet least understood, subjects in our society. To get an idea of how widespread stress problems are, just look at the number of tension relievers on the shelf at your corner drugstore. The market for aids to relaxation must be tremendous to attract so many brands to the competitive marketplace.

WHO SUFFERS FROM STRESS?

What kind of person would you say suffers most often from the symptoms of stress? Most people would answer, the hard-driving business executive, the highly motivated salesperson, or the nervous financial investor. But, according to the National Institute of Mental Health, they would be wrong.

At least, they'd be wrong if you can consider the symptoms of stress. One of the major symptoms of stress and distress is dependence on tranquilizing drugs and alcohol. The NIMH reports that the group that most commonly abuses drugs and alcohol is middle-aged housewives. Another symptom of stress and distress is suicide. Again, the NIMH figures are surprising. They report that the two groups that take their own lives most often are the very old and people between the ages of 18 and 25. Depression is another symptom of stress and distress. Would you believe that the NIMH says that one out of every five children in America is suffering from serious depression? (If you are chronically depressed, depend seriously on drugs or alcohol, or have seriously considered taking your own life, talk with your physician or a professional counsellor about it right away).

Before you jump to the conclusion that those of us who are busily pursuing careers are safe from the effects of stress and distress, consider this fact. A high percentage of the victims of hypertension (high blood pressure) and heart attack are the highly motivated people in industry and community leadership.

What does all this mean? All of us—regardless of age, sex, career, financial status, race, or educational level—are subject to the effects of stress.

WHAT CAUSES STRESS?

In the daily experience of life, all of us encounter stress-inducing events and circumstances. Someone said, "The problem with life is that it is so daily!"

Every day we are confronted with factors that produce tension or stress. Here are just a few of the common ones:

- Changes in an important area of our lives.
- Dull and uninteresting routine.
- Conflicts with the people we love or the people we work with.
- Threats to our security.
- Personal loss through death, divorce, or separation.

- Physical ailments.
- Success.
- Pregnancy and the birth of a child.

These, and many other stress-inducing factors, present a tremendous challenge to us as we reach out for success. The person who is not distressed is the person who has learned to cope with stress effectively. Most people can avoid distress by learning to effectively control stress in the daily experience of life. Here are some tips on handling tension and stress:

TIP 1
Learn How to Cope with Change

A change in job status, in residence, in marital relationship, or in any significant area of your life usually produces stress. When such changes occur in bunches—like bananas—they can produce tension and distress. Since changes occur frequently for most of us, it is important that we learn to accept them as challenges and opportunities to grow. These two pointers can help us to do that:

1. Accept the fact that your life will change constantly, and practice adapting to it. Learn to make an adventure of adjusting to new situations and challenges.
2. Keep your eye on your long-range goals and values.

A Navy jet pilot once told me that, at first, he was terrified at having to land his aircraft on the deck of an aircraft carrier. "Everything was in motion," he said. "The ship was tossing up and down, the waves were moving, the airplane was moving. Trying to get it all to move together seemed impossible." Sometimes life seems like that, doesn't it?

An old pro gave the young pilot some advice that solved the problem. "There is a yellow marker in the center of the flight deck that always stays still. I always line up the nose of the plane toward that mark, and fly straight toward it," said the old veteran.

That's pretty good advice for coping with change—and with stress. Always have a goal to work toward, and keep your eyes fixed firmly on it.

Tip 2
Learn to Cope with Problems

A most helpful statement is this: "Every problem has a solution—including this one!" There is nothing positive in denying the existence of problems. On the other hand, some of the most successful people in the world are those who went looking for problems, then found ways to solve them. Here are eight ways you can turn problems into adventures—before the stress they cause leads you to distress:

1. *Plan for problems.* For example, I do not "expect" to have a flat tire, but I always carry a spare tire in the trunk of my car. I'll bet you do too! Learn to be prepared with most problems that could arise.

2. *Meet problems with courage, faith, and hope.* Problems are usually opportunities hiding behind a frightening mask. When you meet them with faith, hope, and courage, you can turn them into steppingstones on the road to your goals.

3. *Confront problems—don't avoid them.* One of the greatest evidences of wisdom is the ability to recognize, and solve, a problem before it becomes an emergency. Two salesmen were sent to primitive areas of Africa to sell shoes. One salesman took an immediate flight home because the natives didn't wear shoes. The other wired his company: "Send millions of shoes in all sizes, quick. Natives have no shoes!"

4. *Make sure you understand the problem.* One reason problems don't get solved is that we often don't understand the true nature of the problem. "Johnny fell into the lake," the little boy excitedly said to his mother. "Did you give him mouth-to-mouth resuscitation, as I taught you?" she asked. "I tried to," replied the chagrined little fellow, "but he kept jumping up and running away!" Always write down a simple statement of the problem. You might discover that what you have perceived as the problem is only a symptom of the real problem.

5. *Examine the problem by asking questions.* Don't jump to conclusions without seeing the problem in its total context. The solution always lies in fixing the problem—not fixing the blame. As you ask questions, often you will find solutions beginning to emerge.

6. *Formulate several possible solutions.* Have an objective in mind before you start. Simply state what the situation will look like when the problem is solved. List all reasonable choices open to you. Selecting an option is usually easier than coming up with a solution. Also, talk the problem over with someone whose judgment you value.

7. *Choose a solution and act.* If a big step is called for, take it. Two small steps won't get you over a chasm. It is usually better to make a mistake than to do nothing or to postpone action.

8. *Turn your back on the problem and your face toward your next challenge.* Losers wallow in their problems, but winners shift gears and keep going. Some solutions might take years to implement. You might even have to adjust your proposed solution to accommodate new information—but don't quit!

Tip 3
Learn to Deal with Conflicts

All of us have conflicts within ourselves, with other people, and with the organizations we work for. Psychologists tell us that people seek to cope with those conflicts in basically six ways:

1. We withdraw. We simply walk (or run) away from the conflict.
2. We lapse into indifference. We refuse to get involved, and find ways to get around unpleasant situations.
3. We compromise. We seek to negotiate solutions in which everybody wins.
4. We seek help from a third party. Counsellors and arbitrators are asked to help with resolving the conflict.
5. We get locked into a win/lose struggle. People come to blows; they identify each other as enemies. Usually the stronger one prevails—at least temporarily. Ultimately, everyone loses.
6. We engage in creative searches for solutions to the conflict.

It's easy to look at that list and select the methods of dealing with conflict that are most productive. Of course, you can use a combination of several of them. Whatever methods you use, deal with conflicts effectively, because unresolved conflicts become one of the most frequent causes of stress and distress.

Tip 4
Conquer the Worry Habit

Worry is a common problem, and it is a real killer. Worry can sap your creative energies, it can make you less effective, and it produces no positive results. Are you like the fellow I met recently? He said, "I worry a lot about the fact that I worry so much." Norman Vincent Peale offers these steps to conquer worry.

- First, state the problem. Seek to clearly understand what is worrying you.
- Second, try to determine the likely consequences of the problem, and decide a course of action to deal with those consequences.
- Third, try to project the worst thing that could come out of the problem. Usually, it is much less severe than we tend to think when we are caught up in worrying about it.
- Finally, set about working toward ways of reducing the worst possible consequences. Get to work on solving the problem.

People worry for only two reasons. Either they stand to lose something they want to keep, or they stand not to gain something they want. If keeping something you have costs you your peace of mind, or if something you stand to gain takes you to the brink of distress, it makes sense to ask yourself whether what you are worried over is worth the price.

Conquer the worry habit, and you can reduce your chances of distress. Don't worry about it— do it!

Tip 5
Learn How to Relax and Relieve Tension!

Dale Carnegie told the story of two men who were out chopping wood. One fellow worked hard all day, took no breaks, and only stopped briefly for lunch. The other chopper took several breaks during the day and a short nap at lunch. At the end of the day, the woodman who had taken no breaks was quite disturbed to see that the other fellow had cut more wood than he had.

"I don't understand," he said, "Everytime I looked around you were sitting down—yet you cut more wood than I did."

"Did you also notice that while I was sitting down, I was sharpening my ax?" his companion asked.

Mr. Carnegie, who was widely known as one who got a lot of work done every day, used that story to illustrate the need to rebuild one's energies through relaxation.

I would recommend these suggestions for relaxing and relieving tension:

1. Take a short relaxation or meditation break periodically.
2. Vary your tasks from time to time. Working too long in a single position or one one task not only reduces your productivity but also produces stress.

3. Exercise vigorously every day. Doing so helps you to relieve tension, and you'll sleep better at night. One doctor recommended that you always see to it that your body is as tired as your mind at the end of each day.

4. Practice emptying your mind each night as you prepare for bed. Remind yourself that you have done all you could do that day, and you have your plans in order for the next day.

Tip 6
Learn to Keep Events in Perspective

Learn to separate what is really serious from what is merely frustrating. Most of the things we call serious are really only annoyances. For example, an attorney was late for an appointment and explained that his car had broken down on the way.

"I hope it was nothing serious," said his client.

"How can it be serious?" asked the attorney, "It's only a car."

Tip 7
Cultivate a Good Sense of Humor!

Stress seldom overcomes people who can laugh at their problems and at themselves. Learn to look for the humor in every situation—you'll live longer and have a lot more fun. Some of the best stress-relieving medicine I ever found came in the form of a piece of advice. Someone said, "Don't take yourself too seriously—or nobody else will!"

Tip 8
Vary Your Interests!

"Take time to smell the roses." This old saying is as valid today as the day it was first spoken. The time you spend enjoying your family, your friends, your hobbies, and your cultural interests will not only make your life richer, but also help you to cope with stress.

Practice these eight tips to help you handle stress and prevent distress, and your life will never fall victim to tension and stress.

Exercise 14 –1. Dealing with Tension.

Make a list of the five most common sources of tension in your life. Once your list is made, follow each of these steps:

1. Put a check mark by each thing on the list that you can change, and an "X" beside each one you cannot change.
2. Make a list of strategies for changing each of the things you have checked that you feel you can change.
3. Make a list of strategies for coping with each thing on your list that you put an "X" beside because you felt it could not be changed.

chapter fifteen
HOW TO
AVOID BURNOUT

Once a man climbed the ladder of success until he reached the very top—*then he jumped off*!

A new word is creeping into our language: "burnout." The old definitions of the term give a couple of strong clues that can help us understand the new meaning. One dictionary defines burnout as, "the cessation of operation of a jet or rocket engine—usually from the exhaustion of fuel." Another dictionary defines burnout as, "the cessation of operation of a jet or rocket engine—usually from the exhaustion of fuel." Another dictionary defines out of fuel, or soil burned up by excessive heat?

Of course this word has been around for some time, but it is taking on new meaning from psychologists and industry leaders. Career burnout has been defined as feelings that your job no longer holds excitement, risk, or reward. In other words, people who are suffering from burnout run out of fuel; they become unresponsive and apathetic. They are a little like the lady who said, "I'm neither for nor against apathy."

BURNOUT STARTS EARLY

If you are a young charger, you might be tempted to put this chapter away until you reach middle age, and face what some call a "midlife crisis." Yet psychologists are discovering that the seeds of burnout are sown in early adulthood, while young women or men are setting goals for life, investing themselves completely in pursuit of those goals, and establishing relationships that will last a lifetime. Psychologists are also discovering that more and more people are burning out in their late twenties and early thirties.

The tragedy is that burnout affects far more people than it should. The beautiful model finds out that her career is over by the time she reaches thirty. The middle-aged executive is fired during the year he expected to become president of the company. Or the deeply depressed senior person cannot cope with forced retirement. For these people, burnout is serious business.

You can avoid burnout! Many people do. Here are some pointers on how you can avoid the loss and pain of burnout.

WHY DO PEOPLE BURNOUT?

Why do people burn out? Because our feelings are so individualized, there are about as many reasons for people burning out as there are people. But all of those reasons can be put into two basic categories.

1. People burn out because they fail to reach their goals.
2. People burn out because they reach their goals and are disappointed.

Failing to Reach Your Goals

People fail to reach their goals in life for many reasons—some of them completely beyond their control. In Authur Miller's famous play, *The Death of a Salesman*, Willy Loman was always going to make the "big sale" that was going to make him rich and famous, but he died a pathetic, defeated person. Here are some of the most common reasons people fail to reach their goals:

- Their goals are unrealistically high.
- They suffer unexpected injuries or illness.
- They fall victims to circumstances beyond their control. For example, a company is sold or goes out of business, a new machine makes their job skill obsolete, or they lose large amounts of money during a stock market crash.
- People also fail to reach their goals because they don't work hard enough or they make a series of bad decisions.

Whatever the reason, the result of failing to reach goals can be burnout—a loss of a sense of meaning and purpose, a loss of enthusiasm and drive, and a feeling of hopelessness and despair.

Did you notice that I said the result "can be" burnout? It doesn't have to be. We will talk more later about how you can avoid burnout.

Disappointment Upon Reaching Your Goals

Here are some of the more common reasons people are disappointed in reaching their goals—like the fellow who climbed the ladder of success and jumped off:

- They set goals that are too low. A person might decide to become a millionaire and, by the time he is thirty, he has already passed that landmark.
- A person is often disappointed because his or her goals do not satisfy the needs they had expected them to meet. For example, people who look to their careers to solve all their personal problems are often disappointed. No matter how successful they become, the personal problems continue to plague them.
- Others do not recognize their achievements as worthwhile. Family members often have totally different goals—like the son who says, "I know you worked hard, Dad, but I don't want to go to college!"
- They find their goals too narrow. A person who invests all of his energies and time in a career may find that when the career is over, there is nothing left to live for.

Whether you fail to reach your goals, or reach your goals and find them disappointing, the result can be the same—burnout!

HOW TO AVOID BURNOUT

How can you avoid burnout? Or how can you deal with burnout if you are already experiencing it? People facing burnout have three options:

1. They can drop out psychologically, maybe even physically.
2. They can fight back at the institution or people whom they feel have done this to them.
3. They can search for a revival of purpose.

Dropping Out

People who drop out psychologically become passive, unresponsive, apathetic—or they withdraw into a fantasy world. Willy Loman tried to deal with his burnout this way. Right to the very end, he talked about how many important people he knew. "Just wait until my funeral," he told his wife and children, "You'll see how many people show up to send me off!" But the "important people" never came. When a person chooses to drop out, everybody loses.

Fighting Back

People who choose to fight back blame their frustrations and problems on other people—or maybe on the institutions they have given themselves to. But they only increase their hurt and anger, and sometimes they damage the relationships that mean most to them.

Searching for a Revival of Purpose

People who choose this option often find that their new purposes have more meaning and reward than their original goals. The best way to avoid burnout is to learn, early in life, the secret of redirection. This option might mean "taking space from work" to pursue some interest you've always put off. It might mean a career change, a change of residence, or learning a new skill.

Most often, redirection means rediscovering the sources of meaning that lie within yourself or close at hand. *Acres of Diamonds* is one of the most beautiful books I ever read. It tells the story of a man who sold his property, said goodbye to all his friends, and set out to find the most valuable commodity he knew—diamonds. Many years later he returned, broke, old, and disillusioned at his failure. As he went to visit his old homeplace, he discovered that it was bustling with activity. The backyard he had left had become one of the largest mines in the world. The new owners were mining acres of diamonds.

People who learn how to redirect often find that the spouse they had long neglected is the dream companion they have sought for. A person who has always been money-oriented might discover new meaning by offering free community service. Someone has said that the person who is successful in only one area of life is a failure. If you would avoid burnout, keep reaching up—keep reaching out.

SYMPTOMS OF BURNOUT

Are you suffering from the symptoms of burnout? Here's a list of ten questions that might help you to make some interesting discoveries:

1. Do you feel yourself under pressure to perform *all* the time?
2. Do you have to work harder to generate excitement enough to keep from being bored?
3. Does one area of your life drain most of your energies?
4. Do you feel a lack of intimacy with the people around you?
5. Do you find it hard to relax?
6. Are you inflexible once you have taken a stand on something?
7. Do you identify so closely with your activities that if they fall apart, you do too?
8. Are you always worried about preserving your image?
9. Do you take yourself too seriously?
10. Are you increasingly irritable? More and more short-tempered? More disappointed in the people around you?

Are you satisfied with the answers you gave? If you feel, based on your answers, that things are going pretty well, I would suggest that you focus on avoiding those traps that can lead you into burning out. If you answered "yes" to as many as four of the questions, you might be a candidate for burnout. Let me suggest that you back up and review the questions. Once you've thought about your answers, ask yourself if this is how you want to be. Is it how you started out being? If not, when did things change? Are you in charge of your life? Or has it taken charge of you?

Burnout is reversible—no matter how far along it is. If you feel burned out, seek to redirect your energies and find new meaning. The following "principles to live by," from Og Mandino's inspiring books, can help you do just that. My friend Og, who served on my board of directors when I was president of the National Speakers

Association, prefaces his list of principles with the statement that they are based on the premise that tomorrow never comes. We must therefore make the most of today. Here are the principles:

1. Today I begin a new life—I will fill my mind with good thoughts.
2. I will greet this day with love in my heart—I will make love my greatest weapon.
3. I will persist until I succeed—I was not born into this world for defeat; I was born to win.
4. I am nature's greatest miracle—I will believe myself.
5. I will live this day as if it is my last.
6. I will be master of my emotions.
7. I will laugh at the world—I will stop taking others and myself too seriously.
8. Today I will multiply my value a hundredfold.
9. I will act now—I will not practice procrastination.
10. I will pray—When I pray, my cries will only be cries for guidance.

We were not created to do anything that we cannot do with everything within us. And age has little to do with it! A dentist in Duluth, Minnesota, has more patients at age 89 than ever in his life. His hands are still steady, and he is considered competent by his peers. "I'll quit when they carry me up the hill—feet first," he told a reporter. Contrast that attitude with the young man (in his early twenties) who told his counsellor that the first thing he did upon awakening each morning was to try to "find one good reason to get out of bed."

The really great people never cease to grow.

- Bismark, who died at 83, did his greatest work after he was 70 years old.
- Titian, the celebrated painter, worked right up to his death at age 99.
- Goethe finished *Faust* a few years before he died, at 83.
- Gladstone took up a new language when he was 70.
- Lapland, the astronomer, died at 78, crying, "What we know is nothing; what we do not know is immense!"

Let yourself grow, and grow, and keep on growing—spiritually, professionally, mentally, and in all your relationships. Follow the great characters of the past. "If I have seen farther than others," said Sir Isaac Newton, "it is because I have stood on the shoulders of giants."

BE THANKFUL FOR YOUR BURDENS

If it were not for the things that go wrong in your work, for the difficult people you have to deal with, for the burden of the decisions you have to make, and for the responsibility you carry, a lesser person could do your job at about half of what you make. When the truly great people discover that they have been deceived by the signposts along the road of life, they just shift gears and keep on going.

"Hope is greater than history," said Dwight Morrow in his famous one-line speech at the height of the Great Depression. And I completely agree.

chapter sixteen
THIS IS YOUR LIFE!

A leading psychiatrist once stated that "boredom is the most common emotional problem in America today." He defined boredom as an "absentee existence . . . always wishing you were somewhere else, doing something else."

"We are frightened to death of silence and solitude," he said.

The psychiatrist listed as evidence teenagers who insist on having a stereo system set at top volume—no matter what else they are doing, the Musak system playing in elevators, and the salesperson drumming fingers while waiting to be invited into someone's office.

Some years ago, each week on a popular TV show, called "This Is Your Life," a person would be invited to participate in a recreation of the special moments of his or her life. I would like to suggest to you that *today*, this *moment, this is your life*! The only moment in which any of us ever lives is now. We may pretend that we live in the past, or we may imagine that we live in the future, but the only moment we ever live is this very moment—the now!

Some people seem to have a knack for making each moment special. They seem to be happy every time you see them. For example, every time I ask a friend of mine how he is getting along, he says, "This is the best day of my life!"

Once I asked him, "How can every day be the best day of your life?"

"This is the day that I am alive," he said with a grin.

Now I happen to know that this fellow is a planner—that he

carefully plans for the future. I also know that he has some special moments from his past that are dear to him. He has shared some of them with me. But he always lives in the present.

SECRETS OF NOW LIVING

Certain people enjoy "secrets" that can help all of us make every moment special.

- First, they accept each moment as a gift to be received with joy.
- Second, they try to use each moment to maximum advantage.
- Third, they plan for the future rather than worrying about it.
- Fourth, they learn from their mistakes, then forget them.
- Fifth, they are awake to all the reality of the moment in which they exist.
- Sixth, they concentrate all of their energies on the task or pleasure at hand.
- Seventh, they simply refuse to allow the weight of an unpleasant moment or an unkind action by another person to encumber them as they move to the next moment.

Another friend raises roses as a hobby and gives them away. Once, when he tried to hand a gorgeous rose to a mutual friend of ours, the friend seemed more aware of the thorns on the stem than he did the rose. Grasping the rose right below the flower, he showed the person how to hold it. "If you know how to hold it, it won't hurt you," he said.

A moment of life is like that, isn't it? If you know how to hold the moment, it will not hurt you. Instead, it will bring you joy.

BE AWARE

Memory experts tell us that one reason—perhaps the most important reason—for people not remembering something is that they never let it penetrate their awareness. They meet a person, and they are so preoccupied with something else that they fail to get that person's name clearly fixed in their minds. Or they can't remember something they read, or heard, because they didn't really comprehend it at the time. *Becoming aware of people, of our surroundings, of what we are doing, or of what we hear pays double dividends.* It enables us to make the most of the moment as it occurs, and it helps us to savor it in our memory for years to come.

Awareness is a strong word. It suggests keen consciousness, attentiveness, vigilance, sensitivity, care, and responsiveness. If you would make every moment special, practice awareness. What is the weather like right now in your life? What is the music like right now in your life? Who is close to you right now? What is special about them? What is special about this moment?

TOO MUCH, TOO FAST!

We are in the midst of a "knowledge explosion," with the total storehouse of knowledge doubling every ten years. It has been estimated that 90 percent of the scientists who have ever lived are alive today. One of the tragedies of our electronic age is that we are bombarded by input from so many directions that we have to select what we will pay attention to and what we will screen out. For example, the typical high school student today screens out more information than the best scientist had available to him two centuries ago.

Yet, with the production of all this valuable information, some educators believe that the average person is grasping less and less of it each year. For example, the three major television networks gear most of their programming to the fifth-grade educational level.

Why do most people screen out so much valuable information? Certainly their brains can contain more information. Mental experts estimate that the average person uses less than 10 percent of his or her capacity to learn. The human brain has an incredible capacity to learn.

If learning takes place in the present moment—in that special moment that is ours to possess now—we fail to learn because we don't get as much as we can from the present moment. The experts tell us that two major blockages keep us from learning and growing in the present moment—two major reasons why we do not savour this present time:

- *First, we tend to be concerned over the past.* We tend to focus on opportunities we have missed, on relationships that are gone, on things we wish we had done or not done.

- *Second, they say we block out the present moment—with all of its possibilities—by our anxieties over the future.* We long for a time that will be more pleasant, we fear a time that might be worse, we worry over something we might not get, or something we might lose at some future time.

Learning therefore has a lot to do with whether you're an optimist or pessimist. Did you ever hear anyone say, as they started out for work, "Well, it's back to the old grind?" Or maybe they said, "Well, it's back to the old rat race." What a sad, pessimistic outlook on life! Yet some people bounce out of bed in the morning, take a deep breath, and say, "Wow! What a great day to be alive. Look at all of the possibilities this day holds for me!" What an optimistic view of life!

What's the difference? Both types of people may have similar jobs, both may have healthy bodies, both may have the same amount of money in the bank, and most things in their lives may be equal. Yet one looks at life as a drag, a grind, a bore—while the other looks at life as a joy, an opportunity, a series of possibilities. Why?

The pessimist has screened out all of the exciting gifts that the present moment promises to bring—while the optimist is ready and eager to receive those gifts. The pessimist is either longing for a better moment, which may someday come, or reliving a more pleasant moment that is long gone. But the optimists are willing to trust in their plans for the future and in their ability to carry them out. They are willing to savor the memories of the past. Most of all they are alert to the opportunities that each moment has to give.

Remember, becoming aware—of people, of our surroundings, of what we are doing—pays double dividends. It enables us to make the most of each moment as it occurs, and it helps us to savor that moment in our memory for years to come. Thus, you have the capacity to make every moment special! And you have the capacity to *remember* each moment!

"But I have a terrible memory!" you say! That is not a permanent condition. You can learn to remember bits of information that will be useful to you later. You can learn to remember events, names, and ideas. A good memory can be a great asset as you reach for success!

Here are five tips that can help you remember:

1. *Desire is the key to remembering.* Take time to realize the value of what you want to remember. Reinforce it by reminding yourself that this bit of information can save or make money for you or that it can enrich your life in some specific way. The more you desire to remember, the easier you can remember. For example, did you ever see anybody forget a promised raise?

2. *Write it down.* Writing helps in two ways. First, "the palest ink is more enduring than the greatest memory," says the old oriental proverb. Second, to write something down, you must see it as a concrete expression. Anything that you visualize is always easier to remember than something that is abstract.

3. *Read your notes aloud.* As you say the words, it will pull the item to be remembered up from your subconscious and reinforce the memory.

4. *Review your notes until they are firmly fixed in your mind.*

5. *Promise yourself that you will remember it.*

An electrical engineer who had a fantastic memory boasted that he could remember telephone numbers he had called only once, and hadn't called in years. To test his memory, someone in the group asked him to give the phone numbers of several of the firms represented at the meeting. He rattled them off in rapid succession, without missing a one.

"How do you do that?" I asked him.

"The key to remembering things," he said, "is to tell yourself that you are going to remember them. Most of us," he explained, "have conditioned ourselves to say 'I have a terrible memory.' It's a simple matter of controlling the mind and making it do what you want it to do."

I have tried his basic rule for remembering and it works!

This moment is special. It has special learning content. Reach out and receive it with all of its potential. Store it in your memory so that you can draw dividends from it forever.

MAKE THIS MOMENT WORTH REMEMBERING

"What happened on your vacation?" the people in the office asked the returning executive.

"Oh, nothing worth remembering," came her plaintive reply.

How many people do you know who are locked into patterns and activities they care nothing at all about? Ask them, "How was work?" and they'll say, "So, so." Ask them how their weekend was, and they'll tell you it was a "drag." Ask them what they're going to do this weekend, and they'll say, "I don't know." One comedian summed it up pretty well when he said, "I'm getting sick and tired of getting up every morning sick and tired."

Memories don't always just happen. In fact, usually we have to make them happen. Here are some tips to help you do that.

1. *Practice awareness of your environment, and what is going on around you.* Theodore Roosevelt loved nature. Often, after an evening of talk with his good friend, naturalist William Beebe, the two would walk out into the darkness and look into the endless universe. One of them would recite: "This is the spiral galaxy of Andromeda. It is as large as our Milky Way. It is one of a hundred million galaxies. It is 800,000 light years away. It consists of one hundred billion suns, each larger than our own sun." Finally, after a long moment of silence, Teddy Roosevelt would grin and say, "Now, I think we are small enough. Let's go to bed."

I fear that far too many people sleep right through the most beautiful moments of their lives.

2. *Consciously receive the love that is available to you from others.* Historian Will Durant often talked about how he had looked for happiness in knowledge, in his travels, and in his writing—only to be constantly disillusioned, filled with worry, and fatigued. One day he caught a glimpse of the true nature of happiness. He saw a woman in a tiny car, with a child sleeping soundly in her arms. Presently, a man came along. He sat down in the car, leaned over and kissed the woman, then softly kissed the child, and the two adults smiled at each other. As the family drove off, Durant later observed, he realized that "every normal function of nature holds some delight."

Share the precious moments of your life with those you love. Make a special effort to include someone close to you in as many of your memory-building moments as possible. Memories are always richer when you have someone to share them.

3. Don't let worries crowd out your awareness. The word "worry," comes from a Greek word meaning "to divide the mind." Yesterday's problems, failures, and missed opportunities, along with tomorrow's anxieties, can rob you of all of today's joys. They can keep this moment from being worth remembering. "To live the greatest number of good hours is wisdom," a famous philosopher once wrote.

4. Stay in touch with your inner resources. One of my dear friends, well known for her motivational presentations, once told a story that illustrates this point quite well. The natives on an African safari contentedly carried the heavy bundles for the first three days of the expedition. On the fourth day, they simply refused to budge. Asked why, their leader explained that they were not being stubborn or lazy.

"For three days they have hurried through the jungle," he said, "This day they must wait and let their souls catch up with their bodies."

We all need that time, at various stages of a busy day, to pause and get in touch with God, with ourselves, and with the deep underlying purposes for which we labor. We need to let our souls catch up with our bodies.

This Is the Moment You've Waited For

If you've waited for that special moment to come along—that moment in which you could find the happiness you have longed for—*this is it!* Seize it, redeem it, utilize it, and make it a permanent part of your life forever.

LEAVE 'EM SOMETHING TO REMEMBER YOU BY

An old man, who was known as a miserly grouch, lay on his deathbed, with his family around him.

"Get my lawyer!" he snarled. When the lawyer reached the room, the old man instructed him to read the will. The lawyer, observing that the request was highly unusual, opened the will and read its one potent sentence: "I leave all my fortune and worldly goods to charity, and none to my family, because I want a lot of people to be sad when I die." What a terrible way to insure that everyone will miss you when you're gone!

There is a better way to make the world know you have been here. It is to leave the lives of all you touch enriched. Stephen Grellet was born in France, was a Quaker, and died in New Jersey in 1855. That's about all we know about him, except for a few lines he penned that have made him immortal. You may have never heard his name, but certainly you remember these familiar words:

> I shall pass through this world but once. Any good that I can do, or any kindness that I can show any human being, let me do it now and not defer it. For I shall not pass this way again.

"He who is silent is forgotten," wrote the Swiss philosopher Amiel more than a century ago, "he who does not advance falls back; he who stops is overwhelmed, outdistanced, crushed; he who ceases to grow becomes smaller; he who leaves off, gives up; the condition of standing still is the beginning of the end."

Get Involved

Each of us has so much to give to those around us, and there is so little time to give it, that it behooves us to make a conscious effort to get involved with as many people as we can reasonably touch. We have much to give those who are closest to us, to those who are less fortunate than we, to those who are struggling to make a beginning, and to those who have given up and who wish to make a new beginning.

Giving of yourself costs little in relation to the rich dividends it repays. You cannot enrich the soul of another, without being enriched yourself. You cannot encourage a disheartened one to try again without receiving new courage yourself. Nor can you give love to the unlovable, without it coming back to you in many wonderful ways.

Trying to give more than I have received is, I have found, a rather pleasant dilemma. So many people have been genuinely helpful to me, over the years, that I feel compelled to respond in kind. But the more I give, the more I receive—and the debt of gratitude grows ever larger.

BECOME FULLY HUMAN

Many people go through life feeling isolated, never comprehending what it means to reach out and touch someone. "You've gotta understand," they'll tell you, "It's a dog-eat-dog world out there! You've gotta look out for yourself." Such an understanding of humanity is as far off base as that of the cannibals who told Mark Twain, "We understand Christianity, we've eaten the missionaries."

Accept the wonderful reality that you are a part of the human race. You and I are brothers and sisters of humankind. Pick up the rythm of your humanity. I like Carl Sandburg's philosophy that the birth of a child is the greatest evidence that God has not given up on the human race. And I hope you'll never give up on it! At times, it may look as if we will blow ourselves into oblivion, kill ourselves off in the streets, or strangle in our own pollution. But don't give up hope!

I hope we can all say with Martin Luther, "Even if I knew that tomorrow the world would go to pieces, I would still plant my apple tree."

Here's a listing of Nido Qubein's cassette albums—available from
Creative Services, Inc., P.O. Box 6008,
High Point, North Carolina 27262, (919) 889–3010.

I. TECHNIQUES OF PROFESSIONAL SELLING

Here's an eight cassette album that'll help you learn all the important basics in the world of selling. This practical step-by-step guide can make you a top salesperson. Nido Qubein calls on his personal experience as a professional sales trainer and a proven, successful salesman to share with you some of his dynamic principles. Packed in a handsome, sturdy vinyl binder, this program is worth being listened to again and again by both the novice and the professional. You'll get these sixteen different presentations recorded on eight cassettes: Increase Your Effectiveness, Build Your Sales Communications Skills, Add Power To Your Persuasion, Work Smarter—Not Just Harder, Manage Your Territory, Manage Your Opportunities, Become Your Company's Field Expert, Turn Knowledge Into Sales, Play To The Customer, Discover The Power Of Asking Questions, Focus On Maximum Effect, You Can Close With Confidence, Close Like The Pros, Turn Objections Into Sales, Turn Stalls Into Action. ($89)

II. SUCCESS SYSTEM

With this eight cassette series, Nido Qubein can help you to awaken your sleeping giant and to excel in your career. As a top professional speaker, Nido has shared the contents of this program with hundreds of audiences around the country. And here for your personal library are the dynamic principles which lead to successful living. This cassette program is a fast-moving, hard-hitting, factual presentation designed for use by a wide variety of individuals and groups. It is practical and meaningful. In a few hours, you too can discover how to possess the magic power of successful living. You'll get sixteen idea-packed sessions including: How To Enjoy A Winner's Attitude, How To Develop Self Confidence, How To Set And Monitor Your Goals, How To Manage Your Time Effectively, How To Be An Effective Leader, How To Motivate Yourself And Others, How To Conduct Productive Meetings, How To Put Off Procrastination, How To Handle Stress and Distress, How To Avoid Burnout. ($89)

III. HOW TO COMMUNICATE YOUR WAY TO SUCCESS

This cassette series by professional speaker, Nido Qubein will help you to reach your potential in effective communication. I will share with you Nido's proven ideas which have brought him hundreds of engagements annually at very high fees. Do you long to be able to speak to an audience without being frightened half to death? Do you want to be able to speak so interestingly that your audience (whether one person or a thousand people) wants to hear you again? It's not as hard as you might think. Many people could do it better if they would follow the suggestions offered in this series. You'll get eight different cassettes including these topics: You Can Become A More Effective Communicator, How To Target Your Audience, How To Prepare And Deliver Your Speech, How To Use Humor, How To Use The Telephone, How To Write Effectively, How To Lead Productive Meetings, How To Listen Creatively, and much more ($89)

——Save $42. Order all three albums for only $225——

INDEX

INDEX